JUST THIS
365

Wisdom and Wit from the
Teachings of Lee Lozowick

Compiled and Edited by

Regina Sara Ryan

HOHM PRESS
Chino Valley, Arizona

Cover Design: Becky Fulker, Kubera Book Design, Prescott, Arizona

Cover Art: a page from Lee's Lozowick's desk calendar, 1991, inscriptions in his own hand.

Interior Design and Layout: Becky Fulker, Kubera Book Design, Prescott, Arizona

Library of Congress Cataloging-in-Publication Data

Names: Lozowick, Lee, 1943-2010, author. | Ryan, Regina Sara, compiler.
Title: Just this 365 : wisdom and wit from the teachings of Lee Lozowick / compiled and edited by Regina Sara Ryan.
Description: Chino Valley, Arizona : Hohm Press, 2017. | Includes bibliographical references.
Identifiers: LCCN 2017013847 | ISBN 9781942493297 (trade pbk. : alk. paper)
Subjects: LCSH: Spiritual life--Hohm Community. | Hohm Community--Doctrines.
Classification: LCC BP605.H58 L6934 2013 | DDC 299/.93--dc23
LC record available at https://lccn.loc.gov/2017013847

Hohm Press
P.O. Box 4410
Chino Valley, AZ 86323
800-381-2700
http://www.hohmpress.com

This book was printed in the U.S.A. on recycled, acid-free paper using soy ink.

Yogi Ramsuratkumar, the God-child, Bhagawan, is the sole refuge of His true Devotees. He is my all, my Everything, my Hope. He is the Divine embodied, waiting, always waiting for His children. He is a heartbreaker yet who wouldn't yearn to have their heart shattered, melted by such a Love, such a Merciful One. This is heartbreak that one prays for, that one treasures as the rarest of the rare of God's gifts to us, of His Graces.

Yogi Ramsuratkumar is my Father.
May I be a son worthy of His Glance.

—lee lozowick

Contents

Editor's Preface

This book is an inspiring collection of short teachings taken from the writings and personal communications of American spiritual teacher, poet, songwriter and performer, Lee Lozowick (1943–2010). From the raw and practical to the sublime and mystical, these quotations touch upon every aspect of life, calling us to stop, if only for five minutes a day, every day, or any day of the year. Lee's words are invitations to contemplation, often giving a new spin to an old subject, and sometimes encouraging a complete about-face.

The title, *Just This*, represents a primary tenet of Lee's teaching legacy. Since humans love to layer interpretations onto ordinary reality, and since most of those interpretations lead to confusion, anxiety and more suffering, "Just This" asserts that we can return to the undefended simplicity of *what is*. Dozens of his instructions focus around learning to unlearn, particularly the habits of the conclusion-making mind. With an appreciation of "Just This" as our foundation, we can see through layers of expectation and fear to make honest and clear choices or enact meaningful change.

Drawn from a wide variety of sources, including some never-before-published writings and notes from his talks, *Just*

This 365 addresses such important topics as kindness, generosity and compassion; good humor and good company; self observation; devotion and surrender to the Will of God; and presence and attention in everyday life and relationships. Not all deadly serious, however, some of these statements strike at the need to take ourselves more lightly. Lee Lozowick had an exceptionally satirical wit, but also loved to make people laugh. He knew that laughter softened defenses, allowing his listeners to become more vulnerable to truth. Many of the quotes chosen here are included for a similar purpose.

Pithy quotes can serve as excellent reminding factors. They beg to be copied or printed out and posted around the house in places where they will be seen often, prayed, or even better, memorized. In the midst of difficult times, under stress, discouraged, hungry for comfort, we can take nourishment—like dharmic super-food—from these short reflections, and courage from these sometimes-fierce injunctions.

The inspiration for this project was the book *Ocean of Dharma* (Shambhala, 2008), which contains 365 quotes from the writings of Tibetan Master, Chögyam Trungpa Rinpoche. Lee greatly admired the dharmic proficiency of Rinpoche, and in fact once asked this editor to "make me sound like Trungpa," in giving her a task of editing his own talks for publication. This injunction became an in-house joke, greatly enjoyed by Lee's students. We knew that his own circuitous style of presentation was often confounding, requiring serious attention to follow. But words were never the central ingredient in Lee's communication. Rather, the mood of humor, expansiveness and deep devotion that he conjured within groups was the primary vehicle for his transmission. People either fell in love with him and stayed around, or found him an "arrogant fool" (a term he used consistently to describe himself in relationship to this own master, Yogi Ramsuratkumar, the beggar saint of Tiruvannamalai, South India) and left. Few remained lukewarm in his presence, and he often laughed with appreciation at this gift of being able to spontaneously "empty the house."

As years passed, following Lee's Mahasamadhi in 2010, many of his students have assumed the challenge of revisiting his teachings, hopefully with widened eyes and maturing hearts. As the master is no longer around to make distinctions for them, they have taken on many of his statements as koans to contemplate, prayers to invoke and litanies of praise to sing. Implications obscured in the "early days" by the brilliance of his physical presence are being reexamined in the light of the radical action needed to take personal responsibility for life and work. This has definitely been true for me, as editor. In the three years that have transpired in the collection of this material I am blessed to have met Lee again, with a renewed appreciation for his vast view and his pristine dedication to the truth of "only God."

While his dharma was theistic, and Lee served in the traditional role of guru to his disciples or students, the quotes in this book were specifically chosen for more universal understanding and appeal. The basic tenets of his teaching will be familiar to those who knew Lee, but the general reader is encouraged to make use of the Appendix for a brief description of unfamiliar terms or for references to particular individuals whom Lee will quote periodically in these passages.

In the editing of these pieces I have taken the liberty of reworking them—sometimes reordering sentences, condensing, and occasionally combining quotations from different parts of the same work. In some instances, in the interest of clarity, I have added a slight definition or made a gender or voice change. All this has been done with the sword of Lee's intentionality poised above my head. God help me if I have modified his meaning, although I take comfort in the fact that he was occasionally contradictory in the span of over thirty years of teaching communications. In fact, he burned all remaining copies of his first two books, for his own reasons, but the possibility exists that he was dissatisfied with the way in which they put forth the teachings that would come to such a pinnacle of expression in his eight Journals and his books of poetry to his Master, Yogi Ramsuratkumar.

It would be a disservice to Lee's work and the impression left for future generations were I to exclude some of his poetic writings in this anthology. His hundreds of song lyrics for his rock and blues' bands, along with hundreds of devotional poems to Yogi Ramsuratkumar, reveal facets of this man, Lee, and his remarkable teaching, in ways that his books, essays and transcribed public talks will not. While he claimed that his song lyrics were not esoteric, one cannot fail to associate them with the encoded song-poems of the Bauls of Bengal, India, a lineage of itinerant beggars, musicians and mystic lovers of God. In relationship to his poetry to his Master, Yogi Ramsuratkumar, Lee always referred to himself as the "bad poet." And yet, when the quality of longing love is used as the essential measure, his words are obviously crafted in the same chamber of the heart wherein the great poetry of devotion has been generated throughout the ages. I have therefore included a number of his lyrics and a scattering of his poems and prayers in this collection.

I would like to thank my sisters and brothers on this path of dharma who assisted me in gathering and evaluating the usefulness of the quotes selected for inclusion here, and for helping with input and design: Anke Olowson, Mary Angelon Young, Karuna Fedorschak, Nachama Greenwald, Nancy Lewis, Tom Lennon, Rabia Tredeau, Becky Fulker and Jere Pramuk.

May this book serve Lee Lozowick's purposes, revealing the raw truth of life as it is. May it inspire radical self-honesty and brokenhearted devotion. May it encourage kindness, generosity and compassion in the lives of all who read it, and support us all in these dark times to return to essential practice in its infinite variety of forms.

Regina Sara Ryan
Guadalupe Cottage,
Paulden, Arizona
July 2017

Note about Capitalization of Terms: The reader is advised that these quotes are taken from many sources, and represent edited transcripts of Lee's teaching over many years. A variety of editors have chosen to capitalize certain and often different terms relative to the teaching. Lee also, in his personal journals and final written communications, capitalized some terms as per his wish. While Lee's own choices were honored in most cases, changes were sometimes made to capitalization from transcribed material by other editors. The reader is kindly asked to forego the expectation of consistency in this regard. Thank you, the Editor.

Just This 365

1

Just This

—

The phrase is "Just This."

Just what?

Just This.

What's "This"?

This is whatever is, as it is, here and now. *Just* means nothing else—no options, no alternatives: Just This. What does that mean? It means that in reality, in fact, there isn't anything except Just This. This is the seed essence, the core of my whole teaching! What Just This actually defines—what it is—is very powerful medicine to combat the sickness of separation, duality, illusion. Just This means no past, no future, nothing else. Just This.

Less Planning, More Skillful Means

———

Seriously consider relaxing and cultivating the skills to meet what arises as it arises without this compulsive need to have everything all planned out—hotels arranged, restaurants reserved, all life's moves plotted, mapped and resolved. The future is highly unstable, unknown, and both mercurial and in fact not here yet, so why try to have it all figured out?

Develop skillful means, lightness of movement, creative ways of dealing with unexpected happenstances. You may well need such abilities, such a capacity. You think you can handle it? You think the future will roll out just as you expect, wish, hope, dream? You better learn how to dance with reality as it unfolds and stop leaning on the imagined reality of your blind subjectivity.

The Call to Practice

Every insight into mechanical behavior is a call to practice. We righteously proclaim the tenets of justice and truth and yet, upon the revelation of our own psychological and personal illusions, lies and failures, we do not act. This is the first mountain we must climb in the ascent to the summit of human potential and conscious awareness. Leave this peak unscaled, and no matter how much "sound and fury" we stir up, we will not, cannot, move beyond the inherent limitations of living identified with the dreams we assume to be the waking state.

4

Prayer as Gratitude

———

We don't have to say the words, "Thank you, God." All we have to do is *live* here and now. Whatever action is here and now, as it is, is prayer.

5

Parenting for Wholeness

———

Children grow to be whole adults by living with whole adults, not by having moral principles pounded into their little heads by well-meaning but unconscious hypocrites. Children are like sponges; they can and do pick up everything that they see, hear and sense, not only in the behavior of their primary role models, but even from casual acquaintances. And what they pick up will influence how they grow up, which in turn will have effects on the world-at-large that we can't possibly imagine. One's relationship to children has an impact on many levels of existence. Conscious parenting, then, is not only about the welfare of an individual, but more about the present and future well being of society as a whole.

6

Stick to Your Dignity

Authenticity is a good way to feel right about yourself and right with yourself, even if others, the blind masses, so to speak, not only don't understand or appreciate authenticity but often greet it with snarls, jeers, sarcasm and even outright aggression of a more physical kind. Stick to your dignity, for in the long and sometimes short runs, it is the only genuine presence of being-nature that the Universe respects and regards. Even so, with the Universe behind you, you'll still die one day, maybe even soon, but don't let death deter you from authenticity; after all, death is not an insult, a betrayal or an unnatural act.

The Radical Confrontation

Although a lot is happening in our lives, it begins to dawn on us that we're not making the breakthrough. "What gives? What's the problem?" some ask. There's only ever one problem—an unwillingness to radically confront the need to cease all identification.

Talking Too Much

Most people are so addicted to self-destructive behavior, so intent upon self-destruction, that they just ramble on until they destroy something—like the mood, space, chamber, possibility, opportunity for understanding or growth or deepening, or the incredibly delicate fabric, or web, of the perfection of what is, as it is, in any moment.

9

Embrace

———

Whenever we polarize with someone else we assume some negative view towards them, the tacit counter-assumption being, of course, that we have "right view" and if only they could be vulnerable to our feedback, input, criticism, they would be working at the same high level that we are. The point is to "move into and embrace" in place of defending (or attacking), like Milarepa offering himself up as a sacrifice to the demon whom he couldn't defeat by the usual means. To "move into" does not mean to always become social and gregarious, to chat the other person, to ask if they need help or to offer our brilliant insights into their "process." To move into is a contextual process, an inner mood, an inner intention, an inner state, a tacit assumption. As long as we have to think about what to do, how to be, which response to advance, we will miss the mark. We have to alter our entire view from defend, blame and complain, to move into, embrace and "accept what is, as it is, here and now."

The Test of Closeness to God

Basically, you know whether you're distant from God or not by how you treat the people around you.

Sustain Love Alive

Love analyzed and dwindled down by petty distinctions of praise and criticism (over and against distinctions of reality, what is, as it is, exactly), compromised by shoulds, coulds, what ifs and buts, is a love unwisely and unfairly burdened in ways love should never be burdened. To love "as it is," as we are, as the other is, "Just This" is to love with *life*. Separate, divide, critique, judge? And love dies. Deep, true, abiding, trustworthy, lawful, impeccable love is so rare that the dying of love is tragic beyond description. Such a tragedy cannot be captured. It is too big, too vast, too terrible. So, do not divide. Do not separate, please. Sustain love alive.

12

Working with Power

As the world deteriorates, it becomes useful to have power, and the more we have, the more likely we will be able to protect the Work and have the Work grow and flow. We will have the power to work more effectively and efficiently.

When we develop some degree of power, we need to understand how few people have any degree of integrity in relationship to power. Often we're very naïve because a lot of people we're around have a relative degree of integrity, but it's relative, because there are still misunderstandings that happen. When we have had a misunderstanding with someone, we don't stop and think, "Am I abusing power?"

When you get out into the world and start using power, people are going to be drawn to it. The more power you have, the brighter you are, the more people flash on that brightness, and the more opportunities you have to abuse that power. The world will be banging on your door. If we don't know all this ahead of time, we will get seduced by power.

Map the Underworld

———

Sooner or later we have to "map the underworld," to undertake the journey of dismemberment; and then we have to be resurrected. As long as there is duality—hope for salvation—there is also the other side of that: despair, hopelessness. When we are feeling hopeless, we have to really *be* hopeless, one-hundred percent. When we are hopeless one-hundred percent, everything changes, because then hopelessness is not provoked by the desire for transformation, peace, etc. Then there is equanimity in hopelessness.

14

Terrified of Transformation

———

How many of us have found ourselves entering into a process of creativity, entering into previously unknown territory (certainly this applies to spiritual life, in principle, on a different scale), and found ourselves panicking; literally afraid that we wouldn't be able to come back? But, if we do give ourselves to our art, or to our lover, or whatever, "we" won't come back. We will be altered, changed, transformed; we will have grown as a human being, sometimes even immeasurably. But most people are so terrified of "not coming back" that they won't let themselves fall into such brilliant opportunities. A secure ego, a mature human being, can allow themselves to fall into a love affair, into deep intimacy or vulnerability.

Losing Self-Reference

At the core of real spiritual Work is the possibility to lose self-reference. You can continue to do what you are doing (be a teacher or a nurse, for example), but let God work through you without any self-reference. But that's exactly what people are terribly afraid of. They believe that they will cease to exist if they give up self-reference. But exactly the opposite is true.

16

Water the Seeds

———

The seeds of being different are planted in you, and they need to be watered, fertilized, cared for in their gestation. Instantaneous, full-grown, fruit-bearing plants are unrealistic. At the same time, to plant seeds and then fail to provide water, fertilizer, and shelter, and to deny the new delicate shoots the appropriate amount and degree of sunlight needed for healthy ongoing development, is a bit cutting-off-your-nose-to-spite-your-face foolish (even if clearly self-serving and ego-guarding), don't you think?

Language Is a Weapon

Language, my God, what a weapon. Vishnu has His mace, His chakra; Shiva, His various swords, axes and knives, but language, though it can't physically crush bones, break heads, carve flesh and pierce organs, how deeply and agonizingly it can wound. . . Language is a fierce, unrelenting and unyielding weapon, devastatingly accurate in its aim, furious in its attack, even cutting yet in its retreat and apology.

I've heard adults who are exceedingly gentle, sweet, kind and nurturing to all except their own children, to whom they speak with impatience, even contempt. I've heard spiritual teachers who are ever soft and compassionate to their students and rough, even vicious, with their own parents and mates. What a weapon.

Language should be used as much as possible to create beauty and joy, not to continue to produce pain and torture. Language is a two-edged sword, and oh, how it wounds when it is turned toward war, division and derision. How divine it can be . . . and, how hateful.

Don't Fix It

You know the saying: "If it ain't broke, don't fix it." Well the Universe ain't broke. Every form of denying the Universe its need, or its urge, to manifest *as it is*—including to manifest each and every one of us in pure and unobstructed resonance, not just in principle but in actual living fact is an attempt to fix the Universe.

Every form, every denial, every neurotic identification, every gesture, when motivated by self-reference over and against Universe-reference, is our attempt to fix what ain't broke. That includes service to those less fortunate than us, the healing of others, acts of generosity and social justice. All the "good" things we can do with our lives, when those things are defined by our illusions of separation and fantasy, are attempts to fix what doesn't need fixing.

Seek the Saints

When the enlightened ones throughout history have been asked how to realize truth they have invariably said, "Seek the company of saints." That is *satsang*. Why not follow the advice of those who are in a position to know?

Who's Mind Is It Anyway?

The possibility inherent in doing spiritual work is that we may sever the tendency to identify personally with every impression of mind that arises in us. It is possible to stop defining every impression that occurs as good or bad, and to stop trying to redo the "bad" ones, because really they never end. Even if you resolve the ones that you picked up in this life, if reincarnation is a fact you've got all the negative impressions of all your other lives to account for. It is very important to understand something: If there is only God, and if we are all actually connected to one another, then without some superhuman capability it would be impossible to tell whether the impressions that run through your mind are yours or anybody else's. If we can't purify our own psychology, it's ridiculous to think about dealing with the psychological accumulations of vast cultures of which we know absolutely nothing.

What Else Is Practice Good For?

Practice establishes context, habit, matrix. You can't build a building on a foundation of sand, or it will just fall over. You've got to have a solid foundation. If you're building in an area where earthquakes are possible then you can't just have any foundation, you have to have a very particular foundation that's designed to adjust when there's an earthquake so the building just doesn't fall over. Life is the same way. Practice builds foundation out of which we can live with stability, with certainty, with strength, with consistency.

Destruction Awaits

———

This dirty Beggar, Yogi Ramsuratkumar, is no common saint. Love is no respecter of culture, or of personal limits, and in knowing no limits it destroys everything in its path. And Love is something that Yogi Ramsuratkumar is a Master of. And He will destroy you if you let Him, and sometimes even if you don't know you're letting Him. What will be destroyed? Illusion. Ego. Misery. Blindness. Selfishness. Cruelty. Greed. Is the ageless goal of union with God—which we might call the final and permanent shattering of the illusion of separation— worth the complete surrender, even the obliteration of all you now know, feel, think, and assume? This "bad poet," Lee, says yes, and not just yes, but yes without question.

23

Questioning Everything

———

Everything that arises falls into the same category, which is *not* who we are. Everything that arises—happiness, joy, delight, wonder, as well as sorrow, guilt, shame, greed, vindictiveness, violence, aggression and so on. All of it. We like and we want to keep the things that are pleasant, and we don't like and want to get rid of the things that are unpleasant. When we try to practice Enquiry, what we usually do when something uncomfortable—something we don't like—arises we say, "Who am I kidding?" [the form of Enquiry suggested by Lee for his students] because we want to pierce that discomfort. But when something we like arises, we don't question it because we don't want to pierce it. We want it to stay because it's pleasant. The thing about Enquiry is that you have to question everything across the board without distinction and without discrimination. Otherwise you get a biased view; otherwise the one who is questioning is the same one who is maintaining the illusion. At some point the question has to come from source, from consciousness and not from mind, but in the beginning it's only ego. So, we start with ego.

A Dinosaur for the Work

I admit it: I am a dinosaur. It's not that I'm stupid because I choose to maintain my computer illiteracy and stay technologically backwards, it's that I prefer the "human" approach. I want to see the people I'm talking to. I want to know my "followers" personally, directly. I fully realize that I am possibly skimping on my responsibility to make the Work as fully accessible as I can, and yet, and yet… I still enjoy the intimacy of live contact, face to face, contained by a common space. This e-mail mentality, the impersonality of it, is abhorrent to me. I'll stay with the old-fashioned way, an adherent to essence over utility. Yes, I'm just a dinosaur, I know, and none-the-less (or more-the-less) I will continue doggedly on this Path, valuing, deeply, the human touch, the human contact, the human "elan vital."

Learn to Serve

If you want to learn how to serve people, you don't go to therapy and deal with your inner child; you learn how to serve people by serving people. After a while you start to realize that you can serve anybody, including the people you don't want to serve, with the same degree of commitment, because service is not about personality. If service was about personality, the only people we'd ever serve would be the very small number of people whose personalities don't irritate us.

26

Grateful for Everything

———

It is natural for the human ego or mind to be so enamored with itself and its own powers that it expects God to bow down to it and give it what it wants. But the "beggar" assumes he or she deserves nothing and then every gift is pure Benediction.

"I Am Meditation"

Ramana Maharshi was a great saint. He had a gentle, sweet appearance, very refined. He'd been teaching for thirty years, and somebody asked him how much time a day he spent meditating. He laughed and said, "I don't meditate, I am meditation." Ultimately, the quality of mind that we discover when meditation has begun to become essential is present all the time, twenty-four hours a day, waking and sleeping. In aikido, for instance, if one is going to become a serious practitioner, at some point there needs to be a shift from thinking about the response to an attack to responding spontaneously. The only way to do that is to bypass the mind because by the time the mind has designed a response to an attack, you're already on the ground and you're dead! The state of consciousness out of which the body responds spontaneously is the state of meditation.

No Utopia Here

It might have seemed to some few of you that the Way was about finding some utopian otherworldly "spiritual" Eden and establishing ourselves there, buffered and protected from all and any "mishaps." I think not. We live in a world in which the texture of life includes a vast variety of circumstances, and these circumstances are not a test to see what kind of practitioners we are. It is simply life-as-it-is, Just This, meant to be recognized clearly, not avoided but actually respected as a part and parcel of the stream we have entered in order to Realize and Transform.

Rare Beauty

Real objective beauty is incredibly rare, so if it happens once in awhile, it's worth everything. It's worth surrendering one's life in pursuit of the creation of beauty. If we hit it once or twice in our lifetime—as a painter, as a musician, as a sculptor, as a writer, as a poet—we have paid for our existence.

Simply Practice

The motivation to practice (spiritual practice) is a luxury. Motivation is an affect of separation. When something serves *our personal program*, then we're motivated to achieve that. Practice doesn't serve our personal program. Practice, in fact, is designed to obviate the whole personal program itself. Don't try to activate the motivation to practice. Simply practice. There will be times you feel motivated and times you don't. But even when you don't, you still practice. Consistency is what's important. What I'm interested in is whether someone is practicing, not whether they're motivated to practice. If I'm going to give a student responsibility or authority or attention, it is because their practice is *reliable*. When you're able to practice in that way, your practice will bear fruit and eventually you will realize the value of that kind of practice. The realization of the value will itself be the motivation to continue to practice. But it may be very quiet and matter-of-fact, not full of fireworks and enthusiasm. It may just be very simple.

Years and Years

There are no short, simple answers to the questions of transformation, because the answers cannot happen in a flash; when people realize things in a flash it does not last. We all have realizations along the way, but to realize the fruits of the Path takes twenty or thirty years of rigorous practice with a teacher in a lineage.

Consider Attachment Now

Death. What is it about this transition that we find ourselves clinging, sometimes desperately, to our resistance to it, to what we call life? Is it really life that we wish to prolong, or is it attachment, seeking, sentiment? Even, as many of us have experienced with the passing (DEATH) of our parents, if one is quite elderly there is frequently a fierce unwillingness to let go. *To let go of what?* Our bedroom in the old age home, our enthusiasm for mashed potatoes, our nostalgic memories of our youth? And if we are younger, and have children still dependent on our care, or a loving partner, or a substantial material resource, or physical beauty, or a thriving artistic life, even then, what? What is it that we cling to with such tenacity and even devotion? It is useful to think deep and hard on this question; it may prove worthwhile, profitable even, to figure out these issues, of our clinging, our identifications to our dream images, our wish to make solid the intangible and inherently empty ("Form is emptiness…") so if and when it is our time to confront this phenomena called death, we can respond as adults, with grace, dignity and nobility.

Becoming Nobody

We have to surrender our identification. We are identified with our dreams. "Some day I'm going to be rich, be a great writer," or whatever. We're identified with it, but year after year we fail to achieve our dreams. Life keeps kicking us, "Hey! Hey!" trying to get our attention, but we just keep going on because we're identified with our dreams. It's the identification that keeps us from being the very thing we want to be. It's all projection of the mind! Who are we? *Nobody!* In the Sufi tradition, the only way one can get into the Tavern of Ruin is, when they ask who it is knocking at the door, the Sufi says, "Tell them it is nobody, son of nobody." . . . We keep trying to make ourselves somebody because the mind can't accept being nobody. It keeps trying to identify as this "somebody." Then we come to the Path and hear the philosophy that we have created this whole persona from childhood trauma, but we are nobody, and ah! We've found the Truth! So we take on a new identity—nobody!

Where Is Truth?

As long as you think that truth can be found elsewhere, other than where you are, you are cutting yourself off from reality. You come to a point where you underestimate your situation and view your life as a series of conditionings. Then you think that you need to find reality elsewhere. But you are entirely the person that you are. Not only are you the pure essence of eternal consciousness, but you are also your habits, your manifestations, your thoughts and all the things that come your way. If we deepen the ordinary consciousness enough, then we discover pure consciousness. They are completely linked to each other. They seem different but there is no separation. We separate them through our senses, our perceptions. That is where separation takes place. But inside, there is no separation. There are two points in the same field that come from the same source but are completely linked, in the same field, in the same network.

Negative Stress and Positive Stress

———

Just by virtue of the fact that we breathe, we naturally take in more than enough energy every day than we could ever use. The reason we often find ourselves without the energy we would like to have is not because we don't have the energy, it's because we have spent the energy in uncreative ways.

There are two kinds of stress: negative stress and positive stress. Positive stress is profitable for the Work and negative stress is not. An example of positive stress is when you're working on a piece of art, and you are so inspired that there's nothing but you and the art. Negative stress is worry, obsessing about something, expressing rage. In principle, the approach to everything is to see things in the context of accepting what is as it is, and through that seeing, you shift your relationship to whatever it is you're seeing. On a very basic common sense level, the way we start is with some general categorization in our lives: what is the positive stress that applies and what is negative stress?

Culture Food

———

Most of us have reference points for the use of men's culture and women's culture. Clearly-defined men's and women's cultures provide a crucial, even necessary element in relationships. The nature of a men's culture and a women's culture is not to isolate energies and thus make a clear distinction between the masculine and the feminine. (To make those cultures somewhat exclusive is only a stage that we pass through.) Rather, the nature of men's and women's culture is a matter of nutrition. There is an exclusive type of "food" that men produce for men and that women produce for women, and there's no substitute for that.

"Philosophize" – A Song Lyric

Love is the answer / To questions unasked
Kindness the gesture / To loosen the mask
Do unto others / What would be done to you
The credo of service / To get us all through

Chorus:
Life can be easy / Life can be tough
Yeah, we have choices / But is it enough
To speak in fine phrases / To philosophize
Dig into the mud / To get to the skies

Anger's the poison / That always destroys
Violence, aggression / Just games for small boys
But games can get deadly / As we all have seen
The heart-broken remnants / Of goodness gone mean
(Chorus)

Yes love is the answer / When hate asks us why
We feel so helpless / As years pass us by
Do unto others / The best that you can
With gentle affection / And two helping hands
(Chorus)

Through the Eyes of the Work

There are "practices," and then there is Practice. When I say "Practice," I mean Context—a field of knowledge out of which all things arise. They say in the Gurdjieff teachings that you can "see the Work from the eyes of the world, or you can see the world from the eyes of the Work." "Context" is seeing the world through the eyes of the Work. All of us have periods of that, but it fades back into seeing the Work through the eyes of the world. The mind, in its self-centeredness, doesn't want us to see things clearly; it is invested in keeping us divided and in illusion. Thus, it can take years even to realize that we are projecting our illusory beliefs on the Path, superimposing essential spiritual truths on our neurotic reality. To "see the world through the eyes of the Work" that whole program has to go. To "see the world through the eyes of the Work" is unnatural, because you have to go against the natural process of psychology . . . of personality development. But, that's what is demanded.

Natural and Undivided

The technique is "accept what is, as it is, here and now." It's not, "I have to accept myself the way I am here and now." It is "accept what is, as it is, here and now." To accept what is, as it is, is ultimately to accept the fact that there is no separation. What arises individuated as you is not separate from what is arising as the Universe in its ongoing process of creation, sustenance and disintegration—which is the same as the Father, the Son and the Holy Ghost, or Shiva, Brahma and Vishnu. There is also a creator, a sustainer and a disintegrator in Qabala, on the Tree of Life. If we have an aim, ultimately it is to simply allow what arises to be completely natural and undivided from *what is as it is* universally.

This Precious Moment

All you have to do is develop an organic relationship to the moment—that this moment is the only moment I have to serve God.

Dreams and Illusions

———

You have the opportunity to learn to read the subtle signs, to see beyond the ostensible appearances of the gross outer dimensions, to peer deeply into the actual heart of the matter. And once learned as a principle, as a skill applied anywhere, you have the same results: never again to be dissuaded by your delusions, never again to be captured and captivated by the illusions of your superficial and subjective dreams of unworth and unworthiness, of rejection and un-noticeability. I assume—and it's an appropriate assumption in this situation—that to be able to see the essence, the truth of any matter always and under any circumstances, would be a talent that you would find not only useful but extremely edifying.

Magic, Mystery, Drala

A quality of life that is missing for most people is the quality of magic or mystery. The way we are designed—our critical, intellectual intelligence—is always looking for answers. We want rational, logical answers for things, but in some cases we do not need facts, data, information. There is an entire domain in life in which there are no answers. *Drala* is the Tibetan word that refers to the magic of things that can't be nailed down or boxed in by definition. We tend to feel some fear if we can't explain something, and it blows our minds. But some things, if explained, interfere with the feeling of mystery and magic that these things communicate to us. In fact, the miraculous and magical is happening in every moment. When we discount this quality, this part of life, we close down our perspective of life to a very narrow band. Within that narrow band, life can be pretty okay, we can have good health, a successful career, enjoyment. At the same time, there is a vast, untapped potential in the rest of life that we're not using if we have separated ourselves from magic and mystery.

43

Wiggle Your Toes

———

Being able to work internally with a strong emotional situation (like fear) may take many years of practice. Overall, it *is* better to keep things to yourself and work them out *inside* than to just speak out of hand. But (while attempting to work things out inside) you can do something completely relaxing for five minutes. Go outside and throw yourself in the grass. Consciously tense the muscles and then relax them. Shake your hands and shake the "stuff" out. The simplest approach—which is really a band-aid approach, but it will always work if you need temporary relief—is to wiggle your toes! Wiggling your toes won't in any way make the fear go away, it won't get to source, but it will handle the symptoms, and sometimes, why not? And then, don't stop wiggling your toes until you feel better. Sometimes when you break the actual feeling of fear, which you do by wiggling your toes, then also the feeling of being willing to take a risk will not be repressed. The consequences of a band-aid approach might be very significant. It might be actually the very thing you need to start getting closer to the core of it.

Let's Be Happy

Being happy just because you aren't upset is not the same as being happy because someone else is happy. This latter type of happiness is expansive, and not dependent on lack; rather, it is an expression of strength, fullness, already present satisfaction and completion, not a demanding need for continuation of some illusory game. Such happiness is not founded in the desperation to avoid its opposite, but is always turned outward—a form of giving, with no thought of getting in return. This type of happiness is empathetic, and joyous; it is not empty of warmth and caring, demanding isolationism and protection. This happiness is a celebration of relationship, and a pleasure to God. It is permanent and ever-changing as well, because there is always an "other" who is the reflection of happiness.

Patience Furthers

———

Slowly, methodically, without anxiety, frustration or impatience, "all things come to those who wait." When we are working with people, and pretty much all human interaction could be considered working with someone or someones, patience is a key element of allowing the other to respond in a way that is equally workable. Whether the relationship is between lovers, parent to child or child (adult) to parent, friends, or with co-workers or subordinates, superiors, patients or clients if you are a therapist or healer, nurse or teacher, if we are looking for a certain degree of maturity or basic sanity that does not seem to be present, patience will always affect the situation positively.

A Dedication

To try without the heart means not to try at all. To be alive is the result of a heart that is open and gentle.

Find Commonality

———

Personality is not like clay; it's not that malleable. Personality is rather set in stone. You can round out the sharp edges, you can polish off the dull spots and brush off the dirt, but who we are is who we are. If we're going to work in a harmonious team of any kind, we have to get through our personalities. We have to honor one another's commonality, not react to one another's differences. It's a very difficult thing to do, clearly, but that's the first step.

Just Go On!

———

What to do when you've done something (thought, said) that you regret, immediately or twenty years later? Go forward. Yes, just keep up the momentum and go forward. Do not, repeat, do not curl up in a self-pitying and self-defeating ball, physically or emotionally. Do not, repeat, do not, make excuses, justify yourself, laugh it off or try to repair it (although a completely genuine and truthful apology is often quite useful and appreciated as well). Do not, repeat, do not go into fifteen years of therapy over it and do not, repeat, do not harm yourself because of it, not immediately and not in the future. Do not, repeat, do not "kick the dog" for your own unwillingness to deal with the frustration or self-hatred. Do not, repeat, do not act debonair and above it all like it didn't matter to you. Go on, not unconscious of your action but since there is absolutely no way of redoing it, go on. Enough generosity, kindness and compassion can balance a little bit of idiotic meanness. Go on. Go on with maturity and dignity, if you please.

Intention Creates Clarity

When I use this word "intention" I mean having an aim. The more intention we have, the more clarity we have to observe ourselves. When we self-observe it creates remorse, because of all the time we've wasted not working. Remorse is like rocket fuel to intention. We don't need to know *what's* happening. Intention orients the body toward what is needed to be someone who is intrinsically noble and dignified. And, you don't need an in-depth explanation or definition of dignity and nobility. Like "serving the Will of God," it's tacitly obvious.

Generosity Furthers

—◆—

Remember that everyone works hard in their own way and deserves recompense for their efforts. For us, the tips come from the Work, the Guru's Beneficence or the Grace of the Universe, but for the average person, we are the tippers. So get with the program of generosity, spaciousness and a lack of survival panic around your resources, be those resources money, food or whatever it is, even time. Generosity, not only in spirit, but of physical goods as well, money in whatever form, is a great gift to the receiver and earns us far more in merit or karma points, so even though the payback may take some time, in rare cases even millennia, no need to be tight, Mr. or Mrs. Stingypants.

51

Doubt?

———

Doubt, so what? Are you willing to take risks, to follow opportunity if and when it calls, to discover possibility? If so, doubt *and* act.

Eat the Teaching

When we receive information, like in a weekend workshop, it's like somebody giving you the proverbial carrot dangling at the end of the stick. It's a gift, but the carrot is of no good to your body if you don't eat it and digest it. Likewise, we all have realizations, but those realizations need to be literally ingested and digested; we need to absorb them and then practice on the basis of them. If you get a headache, and you stare at an aspirin, the headache doesn't go away. You have to eat the aspirin. Spiritual teaching is like that—except it doesn't take fifteen minutes, it takes fifteen years.

Getting a Grip

Some of you may have heard the phrase "a tempest in a teapot." This describes what is a pastime for many of us, and a favorite pastime for a few of us: the dramatization, exaggeration, and magnification of some minor disturbance into a life-shocking catastrophe that we can worry, yell, pout, and stomp around about. "Oh, the injustice!" or, "What have I done to deserve this?" Well, my friends, my allies in the Work, it behooves us to get a grip—in other words, to develop the skill to maintain a genuine perspective on Reality as it actually is, rather than making it into something to feed our life script and fuel our self-importance and illusions. It doesn't pay to waste invaluable work energy on pettiness. Save it for when you need it, and as you all should know, inevitably you will need it.

Here and Now Prayer

When we are living here and now, when we are accepting what is, then every thought and every gesture is a prayer. The way I define prayer it would be worship, or an expression of gratitude in praise of God, wonderful and holy, magnificent, rather than some kind of request: something for me, to make my life better, or even to make other people's lives better. That's supplication. When we understand that whatever arises in the moment is the Gift of God, then we can praise God for whatever is given. Life is the Gift of God, but we don't know that, because we keep trying to mold it in our image. And even that is something to be accepted as it is.

Use Every Opportunity

———

In one sense, we transform ourselves by transforming every obstacle, large and tiny, into an opportunity to practice kindness, generosity, compassion, forbearance, tenacity, discipline—in essence, skillful means, as the Buddhists say. This is the daily Magic of the Blessing Force of the Lineage— not floating in air, telekinesis, materializing objects and dematerializing ourselves. It's sort of like catching yourself as you stumble but remaining upright and on course. Any "mishap" we encounter—from something as mundane as an unexpected traffic tie-up, to an untimely, unmanageable wave of ecstatic Shakti arising just when we need to be meeting an important business contact—needs to be met with an even-handed equanimity, a good dose of humor, surrender, and an embrace of the *isness*, the reality, of the situation. This is life. This is us.

One Aim

———

The popularly held definitions of life, the assumptions of the common man, are so boring, not to mention so outrageously pretentious that they are simply unacceptable to me. I have never been willing to accept the limitation of what is not only reasonable but clearly within the confines of ordinary expectation and I have always ignored the technical definitions that appear to be uniformly inflexible; and, to the disbelief of others, I have created manifestations and effects that have transcended all the apparent impossibilities of the given circumstances.

I have tried to teach, instill in, demand, superimpose on, infuse others with a similar viewpoint or disposition. I continue to pursue this Aim, to somehow communicate to others the will and active possibility in every moment with which to transcend the popular limits of thought, conditioning, educational prejudices and scientific and/or religious presumptions. Such transcendence being one of the Gateways to the heart and being of God.

Confession

———

Most of what we might call confession isn't. It is just taking a dump with other people as the toilet. My advice: don't. I do not recommend any form of public confession. If you need to confess, ruthless self-honesty, kept to yourself, is the most effective form. A good question, a request for useful material or data, does not need to be prefaced with some long confessional story. So, don't.

Tantra Is Natural

———

If a man or a woman is really interested in what sexual energy is and what it means, all those techniques don't amount to much, because the use of them will only make you an energy-mechanic-machine. You will be able to manipulate energy very effectively, even brilliantly, and ninety-nine percent of the people on whom you manipulate it will be wildly impressed. But none of that has anything to do with the transformational possibilities of sex.

Sex has got to be natural. If you're going to do tantra, it should be spontaneous, natural tantra; and if you love someone deeply enough you will do tantra. If you are not selfish and your own satisfaction doesn't come first, even if there are subconscious drives, you will discover tantra naturally in your intimate relationships, and in relationships with friends also. Tantra works between friends.

59

Just Assume It

When I first started to teach I had a shift in consciousness and I knew what reality was. It went away . . . it always does. So, everything I'm doing now is based on an assumption: when I knew what was real, I knew what was real. So why should reality change? Reality does not change. I've been living like that for twenty-four years, on an assumption, and it works! I don't understand why other people can't live like that! Looking to find that experience again is just nostalgia.

Being Communicates

——

How does the Teaching get communicated? Not by preaching but by being. A compassionate, forgiving, and forbearing comportment, actively expressed through one's manifestations in relationship, goes a lot farther to touch the heart of the needy than your words, which are often the wrong words for the person or circumstance.

Opinion Is Still Opinion

No matter how strongly one believes one's opinion, opinion is still opinion.

See Pain As I See Pain

When I look at people, I obviously see two things. I see that people are already enlightened, but I also see that people are suffering a great deal of pain. They suffer not because they have to, but because they labor under the illusion of separation. They are armed and ready to do battle the minute the right word is said or the minute the right circumstance arises or they see the right look on someone's face or the right tone of voice. And they will cut off their nose to spite their face. I will always encourage you to look at the way I see pain, because if you begin to see pain the way I see it, you will begin to see that this kind of pain is not like having an infected tooth. It's not like physical pain. It is an illusion in the sense that it is based on something that is not true. If you begin to see your pain the way I see it, you will cease to have it . . . very quickly.

We Have a Reference Point for Love

The feeling of scarcity of love *can* be transcended since we all have a reference point for communion with another human being. We have a reference point for deep communion. Even if we feel unloved and unlovable, at the same time *we have loved*. Children love their moms and dads and brothers and sisters, everybody and everything. And while it's true that people are invulnerable, defensive, and afraid of being hurt, victimized and abandoned, nonetheless, this reference point for communion still exists.

But, we may not have a reference point for the appropriate response to love or communion when it comes toward us. We may be too blocked by our obsessive, and usually compulsive, drive to get something, that we won't believe it when we actually get it! We do have a reference point for a kind of one-sided communion, and we usually don't realize that it *can be* a two-way street. What we *can* do is the giving out of love, not knowing if it will be returned.

How to Work With a Real Question

With a question, you have to push the question into the very essence of life itself, because if you stop at psychology or whatever it might be, you may get a reasonable answer, but it's not really what you're looking for.

When you ask a question of yourself, you have to make sure as much as possible that it's a pure question untainted by judgment, expectation, projection, definition. The intention is to be asking the source of Life itself, so that the answer is the ultimate answer—an answer that's not relatively true but absolutely true. Because if you ask the intellect, you may get a true answer, but only relatively true. You have to learn to work interiorly, to bear down on the question, to work the question intensely, so that on the outside, nobody knows what's going on. Your question is for you, it's your work, so there's no need to advertise it. You just do your work, and you learn to work interiorly while your life goes on as it needs to.

What We Really Need

It isn't enlightenment we need, it is patience, clarity, objectivity, kindness, compassion, self-respect, faith, generosity, a sense of humor, common sense, discrimination, reliability, trustworthiness, discipline, integrity, impeccable/ruthless self-honesty, calmness of mind, self-control, conscience, elegance, nobility, dignity, perspective, delight, joy, wonder.

Return Attention to Your Mate

———

Whenever you notice that you are being sexually distracted by someone other than your mate, return your attention to your mate; that will reinforce your ability to not be distracted and not be seduced. Keep your attention on your work when you're working, on your mate when you're mating, on whatever your particular job is in the moment. It's very simple and very basic. The strength of your effective attention becomes a source of "food."

It's not a matter of overriding the attraction. Rather, it's about replacing it. You can only do two things with attention— either it's *On* or it's *Off*. If you leave it *On* what you are attracted to, you will be distracted and seduced. If you take it *Off* what you are attracted to, you haven't sublimated or avoided it, you have simply placed your attention somewhere else. That is a very important distinction.

Sometimes, because of the way the mind works, we don't even realize right away that we are distracted, or not paying attention. That's why the Work doesn't happen overnight.

Stop Pushing

The Universe is perfectly organized and always gives us what is most useful *if*, and *if* is the operant word here, we relax and allow ourselves to be receptive to the Universe's timing instead of pushing, pushing, pushing, and letting our minds define the situation or manifestation. And since the Universe doesn't function exclusively relative to a three-dimensional line or time line (past>present>future), the Universe can clearly know what is more useful tomorrow, even if the mind can't possibly grasp such a dynamic and insists on using a resource today, which in fact will be far more useful tomorrow.

Be Softened

To be resonant to the master [or the teacher] we have to be soft, not hard. Whatever in us is hard—pride, shame, vanity, guilt—must be softened. Resonance can only happen when there is softness, vulnerability, not rigidity. We have to be contemplative and allow other viewpoints to be what they are. Often our rigidity, our belief in our own intelligence, will bias us against the very things that could help us grow. So that quality of softness is a primary quality on the Path.

Seek Truth

———

You don't stop being negative by being positive. You stop being negative by recognizing truth.

Be Honest

———

One of the mechanisms of acceptance is to be ruthlessly self-honest. We must have nothing to hide from ourselves. We hide certain things because we find those things difficult or unacceptable within ourselves. Often our lack of self-honesty is simply a function of our own perspective. It's not objective. It may be something fairly innocent, but even if it's something terrible, it has happened, it's there, it's part of our body of experience.

71

Your Life Is Poetry

———

Each of us has certain gifts that we never get to express when we deny magic and the miraculous. We may look at great individuals and feel tremendous gratitude for what they've given us: fine music, literature, poetry. What makes good poetry is that the poetry elicits a resonance in the reader. "Yes! I know it! I can feel this!" But we tend to separate ourselves from these great individuals. Yes, they are extraordinarily skilled and talented, but the common thread among them is that they are able to express the miraculous and magical as it is. Each of us can touch that magic in relationship. We may not write the great poem, but if we just touch the people in our lives, that's the miraculous. Spiritual transformation happens one person at a time, one step at a time. When we have been able to touch *drala* (magic) in our lives, then we touch the people in our lives and our lives become the poem, the music, the work of art—literally. This is not abstract philosophy, but is very real!

Windows of Opportunity

A "window of opportunity," as we use this phrase, is the arising of a chance to do something that in context, directly or indirectly, grossly or subtly, immediately or at some later time and place, serves the ongoing process of our sadhana, in fact of our spiritual life. It could be something seemingly quite mundane, as buying a house or traveling, or something a bit more "charged" like writing a book, or serving the teacher directly in some way, as a driver or in a building project, etc.

"Windows of opportunity" may arise for us once in a lifetime, or with some consistency, and should definitely not be neglected if we are serious, in a relaxed and contextual way, about our Path and our work with a teacher, our teacher, if we have one. And, if we don't have a teacher, the very first "window of opportunity" that shows itself to us may well be the possibility of "signing on" with the teacher who is either "our" one and only, or with the person, the teacher, who will shepherd us until, if and when, our "one and only" comes along.

Life Is Generous

If you are able to accept life *as it is*, exactly as it is, that is the same thing as giving your life to the Divine. When you accept *what is*, as it is, you give the Divine permission to move in your life. Then, transformation happens based on your ongoing permission to the Divine to move you as the Divine wants to move you. Give yourself over to Life, or God, or Truth, or whatever you call it. Give yourself to life and allow life in its generosity and beneficence to shower you with its gifts.

Practice Enquiry

———

"Enquiry" [*using the question: "Who am I kidding?" as per Lee's teaching*] works like this: You ask the question and discover something; you don't do anything about the discovery. Whatever you discover, you Enquire of that, and whatever you discover about that, you Enquire about that. No matter what you discover, you don't stop to do something about what you've discovered—you keep Enquiring.

Sooner or later, you will end up with the phenomenon in which all discreet points of data, everything that stops us— every finite piece of information, every one of which stops us because we have an opinion about it, or want to get rid of it—all just dissolves. The whole knot dissolves. That's how you know the process of Enquiry has been successful. It's not about *what* we discover, but about realizing that everything we discover is insubstantial. What's left? Life, as it is. All insubstantial, not solid. Nothing is food for investigating, opinionating and discussion; everything is food for Enquiry.

Start Where You Are

———

The teaching is meant to be personal—to have an effect on our lives. Some of you are very compassionate and want to bring peace to the world, serve the world and heal everyone, but in fact as many teachers have said, you have to begin with where you live—in the details of your lives. The real teaching begins at home. If you master the teachings in relationship to your personal life, then perhaps in an extended way you can then serve the world. But it begins with our relating to meditation, food, sex, vanity, pride, greed.

A Prayer Before Meals

———

Beloved God, we are in Your Hands and in Your Eyes.
We have no reason to ask of You a favor.
Still, let us be in Your Heart
and annihilated in love.
All this is Yours—for that we thank you.
Even our failure to love You is Yours—
for that we thank You.
Your blessing is *Just This*.
All praise be Yours, Beloved God.

The Gift of Sangha

We have been given the gift of one another, of sangha—an unspeakably precious circumstance. We can either face one another or turn to the side, even turn our backs. There is no neutral. Please, please, please dig deeper into the glorious potential you all have and help to build the invincible temple. We all need a haven now and, Lord knows, will need one far more acutely as time goes on. No one will do this, if not you.

Pain and Love

———

There are only two things that make the poet immortalize himself with the words of God and men, and the artist create beauty that makes even the sun weep for its magnificence. These two are: the pain of anguish that true compassion avails, and the Love of the Beloved that is transcendent of humanity itself.

No Closer to God

We can't get any closer to God than we already are. But we often think we need to establish a place for ourselves in the "upper-world," a safe haven to be closer to God. Your viewpoint is the only thing that makes a difference in your appreciation of your *already-present relationship to God*. Neither the psychological viewpoint of self-appreciation nor of self-deprecation influences how close we are to God. A viewpoint flip *can* happen with recognition that we are already as close as we can get. Stop dwelling on who you are and do your beads, chant the Name of God, Remember God, turn to devotion, surrender.

Sustain a Little Discomfort

I was thinking about how incredibly damnable our search for comfort is. When you are cold, and I don't mean freezing, you are obsessed with the fact that you are cold. That obsession obscures your search for God. I was thinking about how some of you ask about ways of intentionally juicing your sadhana. If you want to begin in a little way that is attractive to God, sustain discomfort for yourself. I am talking about mild discomfort, not extreme austerities. Just in the span of your day, when it catches you, you can work with it.

You As Relationship

"Waking up" is the first step, not the end result. After you wake up, the process is to integrate what is going on into the world, into life, not to say, "Oh, I'm awake. Now I can go sit on a mountaintop or go out in the woods and camp out all alone and not be with people." Awakening does not isolate you, it reveals you as relationship. It is recognizing at a gut level that you are already the Divine, simply present, and there is nothing you can do about it, or would want to do about it, for that matter.

Move Into and Embrace

Even when the "other" assaults us, has assaulted us, continues to assault us, with their failures to "meet us," with their continued refusal to "be different," to soften up, to minimize their self-created suffering, with their ongoing emotional aggression, complaints, pessimism and life-negativity—even under those conditions—that is their business, not ours. It is our responsibility to "move into and embrace" and meet the situation with kindness, generosity and compassion.

Trusting Ourselves, Now!

Part of accepting who we are right here and now is that it does not implicate the future. It is completely and only this, what is, now. When we see ourselves here and now in this moment and accept it, it is only for that moment, but the tendency of ego the thief is that ego says, "You're greedy, you've always been greedy, you'll always be greedy." We have predicted and defined our whole future, as if that was the cosmic statement about ourselves, and we stop practicing based on this judgment. We misinterpret the teaching in this way. Who you are today could be totally different tomorrow or next year. It's important not to fixate trust on a thing. Who we are changes in any given moment, so trusting ourselves is a context. It's not what we do, but who we are.

Working with Polarities

Many therapeutic models assume that we need to synthesize the male and female aspects of ourselves into a consistent whole. But, that's not my understanding. I think that the male and female aspects of consciousness, or being, are absolutely distinct, and I've come to the conclusion that synthesizing male and female is essentially impossible. One needs to recognize what each of these polarities is, clearly, and that recognition will give one the ability to work with the polarities without conflict and to build a being that is bigger than both of them, or either of them separately. (This being doesn't subsume the uniqueness of each polarity, but uses them in its own larger process. Something else *does* get created, but that something else is created because the other two forces, male and female, provide "food" for possibility, for creation—not because parts of those two forces combine to make a third force.) Essentially, the synthesis is in working with each of the polarities fully, not with a literal integration.

Honor or Compromise?

Honor. What a glorious quality. What would we do if we had the choice—when confronted by the loss of everything, yet knowing that we could get it all back or keep it all if we would only play the game that the vast majority of people play—to *compromise*, usually in small and unnoticeable ways, but sometimes in really big ways that we hope and pray, or stupidly assume, will go unnoticed; or, to maintain our integrity, our honor, and in that have nothing left but our honor and the imprint of that honor in the world and in the Universe? Can we, could we, live with ourselves were we to compromise our most cherished ethics?

A Very Big Deal

A few scraps are left after a meal and someone says, "Shall I throw this out?" and someone else says, "I'll eat it tomorrow." Ah yes, but does it actually get eaten tomorrow by that dedicated well wisher? Rarely, yes? In the moment, savoring the delicious flavor of that morsel we have just consumed, we are convinced, absolutely sure, that we will eat it tomorrow, and hence our assertion. But now is *now* and tomorrow is definitely not *now*. And so, true to our lack of self-knowledge, true to our fairly total dis-connection from the reality of our "multiple I's", we commit to an action that we will not fulfill. It's no big deal if the leftovers don't get eaten "tomorrow," or if someone else eats them. But it is a big deal when we, even after years and years of supposed practice, including the ostensible practice of self-observation, fail to be even alert to the small degree required to realize how habitual our mindless and thoughtless sayings are and clear enough not to parrot things, meaningless things (although we mean them in the moment), that we should know by years of self-honesty and behavioral recognition, we will not follow through with.

Agree or Not, Just Serve

One needs to empty out, to empty the vehicle of *you*, of your personal, psychological preferences, demands, and so-called needs, most of which are not needs but desires. You need to serve others radically and dynamically whether you agree with them or not, and serve quietly and unobtrusively (if possible) without saving chits or IOUs that you plan to redeem later. Do you think some people are massively self-indulgent? You think some people are so self-referenced that you'd like to choke them? Serve them, freely and willingly without aggression or hoping they get their come-uppance. How to become empty? SERVE. Surrender doesn't like "roommates"—it likes an empty space, clean, free of garbage and clutter. Empty.

Self-doubt, Not!

The traditional stories of heroic practitioners may be daunting, put-offish, or even frustrating, but they are not meant as yardsticks by which we are supposed to measure our own practice. They are meant as glorious demonstrations of the extents of human capacity, and to inspire us and radiate us, to brighten our view. Yes, there may be great struggles required to overcome our sloth, our pride, our greed, vanity, anger and so on, but these hardships in no way reflect our inability or our basic ineptitudes. They simply ask us to push a little harder, to stretch a little beyond our habitual comfort levels. Self-doubt, as crushing and even absolute as it may seem in its ascendancy is, nonetheless, completely illusory as to its assumptions of lack and hopelessness. It's not that we should cultivate or fall into some Pollyanna-ish superficiality, some rose-colored-glasses hope based on a denial of the real nuts and bolts of this Work, and neither should we see everything as bleak and impossible in terms of the exalted picture of someone who has "gone beyond." So listen: cut it out! Now.

Kind, Generous and Forbearing

I cannot emphasize enough: be kind, be generous, be forbearing, be forgiving, be gentle, be understanding, be accepting, be tender-hearted. I cannot say it enough. I would have said be loving but all of the above are forms of being loving. I could also say remember God in every moment and in all things but each of the above acts, gestures, is the remembrance of God. We all know without question how it feels, and often how much it means to us, how precious and how priceless it is to be on the receiving end of such qualities, to be genuinely accepted, treated kindly, tender-heartedly, generously, to be forgiven and so on, without a bit of aggression, expectation, demand, imperiousness, arrogance or vanity on the part of those who are treating us so. You will never go wrong to demonstrate such traits, such gifts. I could have said serve your Guru, your Dharma, your Sangha, your Path or your practice but all of the aforementioned qualities are that exactly and without fail. I cannot plead this case enough, I cannot in any way trivialize these wishes, so please: be kind, be generous, be forbearing, be forgiving, be understanding, be accepting, be tender-hearted.

Sadhana and Anti-sadhana

"Anti-sadhana" is that compulsive and blindly habitual activity that people are always so busily engaging in, so defensively protecting, and so vitally hoping to see come to fruition in the bursting of the brain in light and heavenly sound. But, all this seeking only leads to more suffering; for even the fulfillment of it is not God, or immortality. Even when the brain does burst in light and celestial song, the individual is still painfully mortal, still dying, still separate and alone and bereft of God.

Sadhana is the pleasant activity that is generated spontaneously and lovingly from the heartfelt knowing that God is already present, and not some future promise or goal to be attained, and that this is true on this plane, after "death" of the body, and on any other plane as well.

Waning Enthusiasm

When the flame of your enthusiasm for the Path mellows, don't make an unnecessary effort to bring the flame back. Don't make it a problem. You look at the situation with clarity and honesty and without judgment or wishing it would go away. Simply say, "This is what's here now." There is an inherent question, which you don't even have to language, which is: "What is this? It's different than it used to be, so what is it now?" If you're able to see it that way, then the answer will come, in one form or another.

True Religion

—

The Work is alchemical; it's transformational. It's a function of creating in each of us an individual relationship to the personal God. Gurdjieff was a very deeply religious man, not in the sense of organized religion, but in the sense of true religion. What he discovered was that there is only one way to "save God," which is by being completely independent of the web of illusions that the world inevitably always has and always will be spinning.

93

A Work Task

———

A "work task" that is truly useful and has real possibility is never something someone can already do, but must of necessity be something they can't do. The idea is to build new Essence habits, to expand the narrow limits of sensory experience defined and bound by the psychological survival strategy of the individual into a much broader and deeper dimension. The idea is to break one's habits and move into domains of true creativity or "invention."

94

Grow Up and Work

———

You cannot, I repeat, you cannot do this work and be middle-class spoiled brats! And we are spoiled brats, all of us. The culture and circumstance of our growing up has seduced and thus misled us. We must grow up and Work.

Prayers Are Heard

We're all fools on a ship of fools. If changes are to happen, they will happen organically. It's not that you'll never be able to do things differently, but everything is a matter of timing. If we try to do the right thing at the wrong time, it's disastrous. So, hold intention without attachment as much as possible. When you have intention you are giving notice to the Universe, then the Universe decides. If the Universe sees it is right, the Universe will open doors in a way that allows your dream to manifest. If not, it's not your fault. People think that their prayers aren't heard when they don't get action right away, but our prayers *are* heard. When we are too emotionally invested in something, rather than calling it to us, we actually push it away.

The Blessed Wound of Love
(for Yogi Ramsuratkumar)

———

Oh, Dearest, Yogi Ramsuratkumar –
    Nothing to say…
    No bad poetry from this bad Poet today,
    only a broken heart.
Longing for my Father in Heaven,
    Loving my Father, my dearest,
        Yogi Ramsuratkumar.
Oh, Heartache, oh! Wound of Love.
    Treacherous? The result of lies you say?
The greatest Blessing, cries lee.

No Instruction Necessary

—

With my students I do not often speak in detail about specific sexual practices. We have talked generally about an approach to sex, but I have stayed away from specific instruction in Taoist, Buddhist, or Hindu tantric technology. One of the reasons is that the joining of man and woman in genuine sexual communion doesn't need instruction. Academically, if our lives were surrendered to the essential Work we were doing, if our lives were free of the handicap of the cramp, if our lives were not defined by the strategy of survival, the highest forms of sexual communion would flow very naturally from within our relationship as a couple. No instruction would be necessary.

Act!

An ultimate truism would be: The world is perfect as it is. Everything is just as it should be. A pathological relationship to that truism would be to shrug our shoulders and say, "I guess there's nothing I can do," which is like lying down and letting Reality roll all over us. What is, is, as it is, here and now, and every gesture we make is an action, so we can't *not* act. To be passive in the face of need is a pathological act. Everyone who has been on the receiving end of an act of kindness, generosity, affection or love knows what it feels like to be *touched* by human goodness. Even if the actor is not enlightened, even if the actor is not acting for the right reason, even if the actor has selfish motives, when the act itself helps relieve suffering, God bless it.

Love Creates Miracles

———

Jesus Christ was reputed to have said: "Love thy neighbor as thy self." He didn't say: "Love thy neighbor *if* they are loveable and if not, reject them, spurn them, shun them and if they don't believe as you do, start an 'Inquisition,'" now did he? Well, at least not in a way that has come down to us through the ages, but perhaps we'll discover another lost Gospel, "The Gospel of the Lawgiver and Punisher." Wouldn't that shake things up? It occurs to me, randomly and with some consistency, that love is a good thing, that loving others is a right and just thing, that love, in fact, Objective Love, creates miracles by the fist full. I'd like to be that kind of love.

Noble and Dignified

Every single human being has "intrinsic dignity and "intrinsic nobility," to use a phrase of Swami Prajnanpad's. Not being in touch with that, we often act in undignified ways. All of us have intrinsic dignity and intrinsic nobility, and when our lives are not noble, dignified and elegant, it's because we have not discovered and *come to live from* our intrinsic dignity and nobility. That's the only reason.

For the Love of God

God cannot be attained, or sought, understood or bought. God cannot be "had" by any sense of the word, by any stretch of the imagination. God may be lived. But how? Only through the most absolute, selfless, and totally sacrificial Love. God, in order to become truly "The Father" of Jesus, or "The Guest" as the Sufis would say, must be loved beyond mind, beyond senses, beyond all that you see and all that you don't. Only Love absolute will do.

You must not even place yourself last if you are to see this God, for you still then have a self to be seen over and against the One, the Beloved. You must lose this stubborn little one. You must not even know "you" exist. You must not "put" yourself at all. There must be Only the Lord, the very Beloved of all ages, times, worlds known and unknown. There must be God.

Supplement Intention with Will

There are times in which intention—as a force, as a field, of commitment to the Path, commitment to practice—is easefully present and exerts its magnetic pull; times in which our momentum flows along without resistance or drag and it all seems almost "enlightened." There are other times when resistance is peaking and we just have no urge, even in fact, an active disregard, for our various transformational pursuits, such as meditation, study, observance of our dietary and ordinary life protocols, even the most basic human relationship niceties, like patience, generosity and kindness to our loved ones and others. It is at these times, the times of shutdown or breakdown, when we need to take an active role in maintaining certain daily gestures of practice. Will. Sheer will. When intention is ineffective, supplement it with will and continue to will until intention—in its mood, its field—returns to inform and fuel what then does not require an effort of will to sustain.

We're All God, But...

Rhetorically, of course, and speaking nondualistically, we are all God: men, women, all of creation. And rhetoric is all well and good, but what about the organic reality that moves us? What about those twenty-five- or fifty-years' worth of denial and other unconscious ego strategies that have literally formed the body, mind, health, and all of our reactions and beliefs? You can't just say, "Yes, we're all God," and expect to be healed, although that would be nice and delightful. But it doesn't work that way. We've got to root out the unconscious motivations and transcend them in clarity and through the disintegration of life negative habits. That is a lifetime operation.

Learn the Basics

—▼—

We tend to define meditation exclusively as a static process—a process where we don't move—and in the beginning it is. Just like in most forms of martial arts, in the beginning you practice *kata,* over and over and over and over and over. Sometimes people say, "What's all this mechanical training for?" It's to give you a container in which the essence of the art can be held. If you want a glass of water to drink you have to have a glass. Or a little perfume: perfume comes in a jar, without the jar, no perfume. Static sitting meditation builds a container, and once the container is reliable then a whole different kind of expression is possible. So first you learn the basics, then after the basics are second nature, then you can be spontaneous.

Clearing Out

Spiritual work is about discipline and consistency, not necessarily about how beautiful and full of light things might look after you've been practicing meditation for a year or two. Actually meditation *will* transform your vision, but not before it clears out everything else that stands in the way. And that process may not be particularly attractive or comfortable. In fact, it may not even appear, or feel, sane.

The Irresistible Name

The Name of God itself entices, entrances and even entitles us. It captures our hearts and makes us fall in love with It, with God, maybe even with Its creation. Yes, this is the power of the Name, it begins as a mere cipher and ends up, again, if we are even minimally diligent in Its own repetition, irresistibly seducing us into Its own sweet domain, into Its own perfumed, palatial, tender, intimate "love-net." So why not? There are only positive consequences, no negative implications at all. Why not?

Trying to Trap Wisdom

We don't need to trap knowledge or wisdom. There is no need to pursue it as if it could possibly disappear if we didn't grab it fast enough and hard enough. The more we try, the more mysterious and frustrating this whole spiritual business seems. It would not be out of the domain of possibility to apply this principle to other both similar and dissimilar matters, using discrimination and common sense, of course. Being too impulsive and zealous, not to mention dogmatic, about exciting new discoveries has led to some tragic spiritual errors, as well as many disastrous relationships.

Transformation of Energy

—▼—

This Work is about taking what is and extracting the positive and transforming the negative. True tantra is about living from the view that all of life can be used for the transformation of energy, from waste material to creative, productive material. Turning base metals into gold requires discipline.

Suppose you have a habit of having furious fights with your partner—lots of energy is used up there. Imagine what it would free up in relationship if anger became vulnerability. What a difference that would make! In principle that is the work we are called to do. In order to transform what is, you've got to see what is. To transform greed or pride, you have to see it in yourself. You have to see clearly. There are two ways to do this: One is to just watch yourself. You notice the flows of energy, when you are high and when you are low. Don't change anything, just watch. The second way is with the help of a teacher (not on your own); ask for a special circumstance that will magnify certain qualities.

Undefended Simplicity

One of the ideas of this Work is to accept who we are, as we are, where we are, and in this acceptance, in this undefended simplicity of "what is as it is, here and now," allow the Divine Influence of God to change us according to God's Will, instead of our narrow view being the definitive perspective.

We Stand on Others' Shoulders

When our heads are above the clouds it is not because we can fly (or levitate), but because we are standing on someone else's shoulders. To belittle, demean, be ungrateful to or criticize, to judge unfairly and condemn on the basis of our judgment those individuals whose shoulders we are standing on is foolish, self-defeating, and ultimately may even cause the entire structure to collapse—for we would not be where we are were it not for them. To be unconscious is one thing (no excuse, but still, what is, is, as it is, isn't it?), but to fail to capitalize on the knowledge, experience, and efforts that have been made by others for so long is nothing but sheer egoism and power lust.

Hard to Be a Bodhisattva

It is a damned hard thing to be a Bodhisattva. Our commitment to service, spaciousness, kindness, compassion, innocence, generosity, and so on, will be reliably challenged, even battered incessantly. It is hard to be a Bodhisattva, sworn to never give up on the vision, of people's intrinsic dignity and intrinsic nobility while dealing, day in and day out, night in and night out, with the onslaught of pain, anger, confusion, destruction, violence, suffering that is so prevalent, epidemic actually in the human domain these days, maybe all days. It is hard to be a Bodhisattva because a Bodhisattva knows that he or she not only cannot, but will not, enter Nirvana until all sentient creature have entered first. Insects, they go easily, crawling, flying, tumbling into Nirvana with barely a gesture of argument, but humans, they fight, scream and struggle to stay out of Nirvana.

Let the Universe Point the Way

The Universe is—how shall we call it?—not a definable object but an existence that is, of its very nature, ultimately intelligent. So relax. That should be good news if you can actually do it! Allow the Universe—or Reality, Truth or God if you prefer those terms—to point the way and send the limousine and simply let it carry you to the effective, optimum, and most profitable end result. And when, in those very few instances, to push is what is needed, the Universe will clearly indicate that. No doubt or confusion is necessary, though we tend to produce both in great quantities and with passionate urgency.

113

Doing Less

———————

Usually when we want to "get things right," whatever "things" are, like relationship, mental stability or peace, or some motor function, we try harder. And usually the key to "getting things right" is to do less, not to do more.

Relax

———

To relax is not necessarily to be less busy but to be busy in a calm way, a non-methodical methodical way, so that everything gets done easily and rightly in its own time and place. It's like one of those little straw Chinese finger puzzles—the more you struggle to get out, the tighter it becomes until you figure out that when you relax it falls right off. It's not that by relaxing we have to stop doing things, but rather that our internal dynamic, that knot that informs us that if we aren't 100% on the alert, in defense against all the imagined demons that will harm us and take advantage of us, that we won't survive. It is this inner tension that is the very demon we are supposed to beware of that is actually eating us up. Before we can actually relax we need to see the reality of the tension. We need to self-observe to the degree that it has become obvious that we are as tense as everyone else perceives and realizes we are. Once we have seen, identified this stress, this wound-up and bound-up internal state, then it becomes an easy matter to relax it.

Unify

How does one discover not only the equality of all beings but equanimity in all things? You don't discover that by dividing and dividing and dividing. The more one divides, the more one is still lost in this and that, good and bad, yes and no—lost in the tension between things instead of the continuity of all things. Assuming that many of us might feel that we love God in some way—whatever we think God is: nature or humanity or the guru or the Path—how do we embrace and deepen and express that love? We deepen love for God by unifying, not dividing. We unify things instead of separating things. When we separate things, then we love the things that we're resonant with and we don't love the things that we're irritated or annoyed by. When we unify things, there is a possibility.

Realistic Expectations

If you have unrealistic expectations in your personal practice, you will be caught in a conflict that is unresolvable, because by definition your expectations are unrealistic and therefore unrealizable. So, either have a reliable practice or don't have unrealistic expectations. You must have realistic expectations, be willing to work as you go, progress as you go and get what you pay for, without losing your sense of purpose and passion for the work that *drives* you. You say to yourself, "I don't meditate every morning; I'd like to but I don't. There is no reason to beat myself up and suffer over it. I'm on the Path, I love my teacher. I'm devoted to this work. I am who I am, and I'll do what I can." Period.

The Greatest Accomplishment

When you consciously love, you can sense the perfection in your lover, not as a human but as an element of the creation of God. No matter what the "shell" looks like, no matter how many good or bad habits the other has, no matter how crazy, you can always sense that perfection, that essence. And, at the cost of everything in your life, even at the cost of sanity, you want to evoke that perfection in your lover. That's conscious love. That type of ideal relationship has to be cultivated. That has to be worked, trained. You didn't grow up being able to do that in this society. The greatest accomplishment we could ever hope for is to become a conscious lover.

118

The Essential Sacred

———

Without the Sacred, and without dignity relative to the Sacred, there is no true life, no life that can be real, satisfying and fulfilling, neither ultimately nor mundanely.

Travel Secret

———

Here's a little anecdote: Arnaud Desjardins, in his eighties, arrives in Quebec after an arduous and lengthy trip and is fresh as a daisy and bursting with energy and he says to everyone there: "Do you want to know my secret?" and they, most of them, if not all, younger and tired-er, say "Yes!" and he says, "Non-duality." Ain't that sweet?

Mystery Every Day

If you look around, if you open your eyes, life can really be quite a delight. There are times of tension, crisis, suffering, but if you were to keep a record of what was positive and what was negative, you would find that about ninety percent of your day is positive and only ten percent is negative. Just getting up in the morning is a wonderful thing. But you forget. You open your eyes and think, "I'm going to see so-and-so and she's going to be in one of her moods." When she isn't in that mood when you see her, yet you still have your negativity.

Life is so incredibly vibrant. There is so much exciting mystery every day. So, to think negatively, which is much too common, is to allow your whole life to be filtered through your negative attitude toward things. If someone bothers you, you may be annoyed in the moment, but when you leave them, you should cease to be bothered by that instead of hanging onto it. When you think positively, you see what is and you respond to it in a flexible way.

No Need to Understand

———

Life has its own Intelligence. We always think that we need to understand, we need to sort through our feelings, we need to do this, we need to do that. But that is not how it works. All we have to do is to step back and let the Intelligence of Life manifest itself. Then everything is clear. We think we need to find this clarity by our own efforts. But if we allow Life to manifest itself as it is and if we just observe it from a context of nonduality, then there is clarity. To try to find clarity is in itself a way to muddle the situation; we think we will succeed, we have the feeling that it is in our reach. But in the end we never get there because we are constantly running after something that is already here. It is like someone looking for his glasses when he has had them on all along!

To Give and To Get

———

Giving without wanting a return is certainly the ideal, but before we realize the ideal we need to deal with the practical realities of life as it is. The fact is that in giving we are always waiting for something in return, but this should not stop us from giving. We should simply observe that element of wanting a return that's always there when we give. We observe it *as it is*, not like it's wrong and we should be more pure; but just as it is. If we're able to do that effectively and consistently, pretty soon we'll find ourselves giving without waiting for some return, and we won't even have noticed the change. To diminish our activity in the present because it doesn't measure up to the ideal is just foolishness. Simply act and accept.

Lose the "I"

We can float in the glow of the Work for lifetimes—irradiated by the radiance—and that's fine, and the majority of students in every sangha do that, but that's not what we come here to do. We come here to resolve the pain of the existential suffering that we feel, now, in this lifetime. We either do that or we don't, obviously; or more accurately, that either gets done or it doesn't. We have to lose the "I" for the touch of Grace to effect this great shift. Most of us are simply unwilling to pay the price that is required to do that because the price is a complete surrender of our distinctions, our opinions, attitudes, requirements, demands. This Path has profound possibility and many great treasures, but we don't touch any of those things if we aren't willing to give up our desires for those very things.

Basic Meditation Practice I

——▼——

The essential form of meditation that I recommend for my students is very close to Zen meditation. Sit and observe what arises, whatever arises—just to watch, not to control or direct in any way, but just to sit and watch what's going on in the mind, what's going on in the body. Do the knees hurt, does the back hurt, do you have a headache? Are you climbing the ladder of mystical ascent? Just observe, just Pay Attention. What's the mind doing? Is it obsessing about bills that have to be paid or some struggle at work, or sexual fantasies, or dreams of glory, spiritual or otherwise, or nothing at all. Maybe you're falling asleep—fine, it doesn't matter. The essential instruction is just sit and Pay Attention.

Fantasy or Seduction

When you are in a relationship with someone and you love them, you are certainly going to notice attractive people of the opposite sex, but that noticing doesn't need to interfere with the relationship. Only if you indulge this attraction will it interfere. Then, all of a sudden, you start fantasizing, finding fault with your mate, wondering how other people would be in bed. Then the relationship starts to break down. If fantasy is simply stream-of-consciousness with no attention, nothing happens. There is no distraction. What makes something a distraction is when your attention is moved to it, taken, or hooked by it. What makes something a distraction is when you give your attention and energy to it willingly and intentionally (albeit unconsciously). A distraction is when your attention is taken. A seduction is when your attention and energy are given. If you don't break attention, you have no distraction and no fantasy. Period.

Bonding Is Important

Everybody grows up from the beginning with one of two primal relationships to life: "I'm loved" or "I'm not loved." That is why bonding with both mother and father is so important. If children are strongly bonded only to the female or only to the male, they may grow up feeling loved, but be personally and psychologically one-sided. If they are not bonded in the proper way, right away during the first two months, they will grow up feeling primally unloved. All of life will be an attempt to get this missing love, even if there is a loving influence. If you are a child who feels unloved, when you get to be an adult even Real love in your life doesn't obviate the feeling that you can't get enough love. In the "I'm not loved" disposition we are always craving for some kind of proof that we are loved.

Lord Have Mercy
(for Yogi Ramsuratkumar)

———

This world can be so desolate when we run
    through it grasping for meaning,
having forgotten You, oh Lord: Yogi Ramsuratkumar,
    meaning and substance
in an often meaningless and empty world.
    When we see this desolation
we fall to the ground weeping and wailing,
    gnashing our teeth and beating our
clenched fists on the unholy ground.
    And lest we Remember You, we are lost.
But should we be Blessed enough or wounded
    enough to call Your Sweet Name,
Yogi Ramsuratkumar, You will our hearts,
    turn our tears of desperation and agony
into tears of love and longing
    and take our hands, leading us
straight to Your Father's Kingdom
    and pouring Light and Mercy upon us.
This is lee lozowick, Your wild Heretic,
    Praising You for himself and for You.

From Self-Centeredness to Other-Centeredness

Nothing should come before the Path for us, but the Path is not separate from life. The Path makes clear distinctions between that which is resonant with the Divine and that which is dissonant with the Divine. Anything that separates us from communion with life is dissonant to the Divine. Greed, vanity, shame, self-hatred, feelings of victimization or vindictiveness—all these are forms of violence. Vanity, for example, is a form of violence because it separates you from the other.

There is no communion in self-centeredness. The Path is about radical transformation from self-centeredness to other-centeredness.

Adequate Is Not Good Enough

"Good enough is good enough" is a principle of my Teaching. "Good enough" refers to the holistic field of its expression, a completion relative to elements of a process in which what could be called "excellence" is unnecessary—an exaggerated or overdone effort that often not only complicates or obscures but even ruins or destroys the most effective or useful results, sort of like turning a perfectly contextualized "spirit of the law" event (or work of art) into no more than a flawless, technical "letter of the law" paean to heartlessness and cool intellectualism, something pleasing to brains with no comprehension of the body's play of existence.

But "adequate" is not good enough. It falls, in some cases, far short of "good enough." Adequacy is actually a failure to meet the mark: a striking lack of understanding of what is "wanted and needed," just getting the job done to get the job done without any deeper insight into the various ingredients of the whole multidimensional, multifaceted system that is being served, worked with, or within. Simply put, to do a job adequately fills the hole but does not fully accomplish the necessary demand.

130

For the Rest of Your Life

———

Someone asks, "What should I do about my fear?" or "What should I do about my anger?" Well, you have to assume that you're going to be this full of fear or anger for the rest of your life. This is the way it is. So, learn to live with it. When someone starts to learn to live with *what is* effectively, what tends to happen is that it changes.

Assume that the knot is always going to be there. As long as you're fighting against the knot, then you're strengthening it. Resistance creates counter-resistance. That's part of the psychology of acceptance; when you accept something, you aren't resisting it. Then all the counter-resistance has nowhere to go and nothing to do, so it just relaxes. As soon as the counter-resistance relaxes, then what is the knot, except counter-resistance? The knot is not resistance, the knot is counter-resistance. As soon as it's got nothing to resist against, then it's got no reason to exist.

The Muse Lives

The creative Source is always wide open and ready to kick ass and take no prisoners (meaning, produce genius) but it is us—the human mind/ego/psychology—that chokes off this ever-present reservoir of brilliance and inspiration. The Muse lives vitally healthy. Our tensions, our opinions, our beliefs, our expectations (or rather lack of them), our psychological insecurities, self-hatreds, limitations—these squeeze shut the channels of "flow." Our refusal to dismantle the rigid and crystallized dualities of possible/impossible stumps our faltering (in most cases) attempts at creativity, or keeps us struggling intensely, even for years, at something that should rightly take little time.

Prove me wrong if you like . . . but then again, prove me right and put your ego where it belongs: under the thumb of God. Stay critical, mechanical and chronically doubtful, or shatter the chains of concept and be radiant in the fullness of your own magical potential, unleashed and mind-transcending in its manifest glory. In a very real way, and as strange as it may be, the choice really is yours, for are you not *That* already, complete and non-separate?

Obedience

———

Obedience is not a blind following uninformed by wisdom, insight or sensitivity to the protocol of a situation. Obedience is an actively intelligent process of submission to a Will (of God) based on Faith and Surrender, and also full of alert awareness of an instinct of rightness, of a "fit" of one's actions to Objective Life, to Divine need. The Divine "needs" our obedience. To "be all that we can be"—without "thinking" about it, simply to be "one with" the dictates of this Divine Will—is why we are created, why we exist. Obedience is not a "lying down and taking it, and taking it, and taking it," when life is pounding on us, but of actively finding an expression of being that "accepts what is, as it is, here and now" and acts in response in a creative, even enthusiastic, sane way that serves whatever is "needing" to be served through the exact configuration of energetic vectors defining the given situation. Obedience is a complete involvement in Life, in the movement of the Universe as defined as the Will of God, a deep, and sober, appreciation for and of "what is, as it is, here and now."

Watch Your P's and Q's

When you serve, in any way, from doing other people's dishes to cleaning up other peoples messes (a thankless and endless project), or in more high-falutin' ways like taking care of an Alzheimer's parent for ten years during their severe dementia, if you, or rather *when you* serve happily and without expectation, you get lots of points. The Buddhists call it "earning merit." And if you complain, demanding or whining about others not meeting you in that service, not contributing, or not appreciating you for your selfless acts, you lose any points you might have racked up. So, watch your p's and q's (pissiness and quarrelsomeness)!

Moved by God

Typically, when people get involved in spiritual work they become interested in the concepts of enlightenment, or liberation, or freedom. They feel the First Law of the Buddha— that all life is suffering—and they seek this work to be free of that suffering. For them, freedom means no restrictions, no bounds, an infinite number of choices. They want not just the world, but the whole universe, as their playground.

My experience is that in real freedom there are no choices…that real freedom is only present when there is "no one" to make choices. When one surrenders to God one is moved by other than one's own personal attractions and conscious perceptions of who one is. Rather, in every instance one is moved by the Will of God. Within that, in every instant, and under every circumstance, there is only one optimal expression for each cell of creation. Anything less than that is simply the expression of ego.

Value of the Fear of Death

You don't need to be free from fear of death. What you need is to experience it fully. The fear of death is very abstract for most people: they don't believe that they are going to die, even if they are very afraid of the idea of death. Death can happen any time, accidentally, or at the end of a long life that you tried to live well. But, *life* is still what is most present. If you really were afraid of death, this fear itself would be an intense motivating factor. When you are not just afraid of the "idea" of death but truly afraid of death itself, you realize that you need to live your life fully as long as there is life. Then it all becomes incredibly inspiring. If your sensitivity to the spiritual process was acute, you would be able to throw yourself into that process, completely, without any parachute. The fear of death would give you a tremendous momentum, would show you how urgent this is. If you truly felt it, the fear of death would make you understand the degree to which death brings the end of everything that is relative.

Adjust, Respond

———

To "live and learn" should not and need not be a painstaking, tooth-pulling, snail's pace, turtle-creeping process of struggle. It should be and can easily be a smooth process of miss the mark, adjust, miss the mark, adjust, miss the mark, adjust, respond.

The Dark Night Is Real

It's a paradox. We live in a domain of darkness with noticeable flashes of light, when at the source of being is pure light. Light and dark are continuous, but from the point of view of duality it seems we have to move from darkness to light. We think the closer we get to light the lighter it gets, but it's the opposite. We live in a vast gray area, and as we go toward light it gets darker until we get to total pitch blackness. If we want one-hundred-percent light we have to deal with one-hundred-percent dark. Hopelessness and despair are very real. Read *Dark Night of the Soul* by St. John of the Cross. "Can't I do it without that?" we ask. No, the way to the light is through the darkness. So, naturally there is some reticence to go there, but you have to have faith in what is beyond the beyond. Where do you get that faith? In the testimony and example of those who have walked that path before you.

Blending Souls

The freedom to be able to offer oneself to another person in a very formal way has a certain power to it. Not in the way in which tradition is just empty and repetitive, but in real tradition, true tradition. Marriage is a commitment to blend one's soul with the soul of another. In the ultimate world of nonduality, we're all one already anyway, and so it is academic. In the relative world, the implications of blending one's soul with another, without compromise, without any withhold, are very, very big—karmically and energetically, and in the sense of the Sacred. Real marriage is about offering yourself up completely; it's literally like putting yourself on a sacrificial altar. We could almost say that the altar of marriage is a sacrificial altar. Each partner offers himself or herself to the other as the sacrifice. It's a sanctified, sacrificial affair. It's not just a commitment of language, or even of the heart. It's a commitment of essence, of being, of soul.

In the Swamp

———

We're in the swamp, the boat has sunk, the swamp is endless, and we're never going to get out. What are we going to do? Lie down in a fetal position? Or look around and say, "Well, I'm going to build myself a place to live; figure out what to eat; make fire; figure out some line of work so I can profit from this situation."

This world is like a swamp, if you haven't noticed. Certainly it has its beauty, but it's still a swamp, and when you get down in the mud and the sun goes down, you can't deny that. So, the question is: How am I going to get dry and live like a human being? Alone in the swamp your chances of survival are very small. But if you are with others who share the same dilemma your chances of survival increase, geometrically. A life of elegance and dignity is crafted out of the swamp, one environment at a time, one person at a time, because we aren't going to save the world. But are we personally willing to live our lives with integrity, as warriors? Because that's what this Path is about.

Err on the Side of Too Much

———

If you are going to make a mistake with your children, make a mistake by giving them too much time and attention rather than giving too little. When your children grow up they'll have plenty of opportunities to realize how impatient and intolerant the world is.

Don't Jump to Conclusions

———

When we jump to conclusions based on established biases, especially when our education relative to the subject is faulty or puerile, sophomoric perhaps, we will most likely "shoot first and ask questions later." Asking questions to a corpse is not likely to be very revealing or edifying. It pays to have the facts about any given situation before going off half-cocked, as the saying goes.

How does one collect the facts? Clearly, a depth and breadth of study is useful, and perhaps more important is remembering to ask the right questions and knowing what the right questions are. We are often so impulsive, and at times too lazy to be even mildly interested in a proper response to circumstance, that it completely escapes us that we may not have all the necessary data or facts relative to a reaction we are having. Remember that we are called, in maturity, as sane adults and intelligent practitioners, to respond in place of reacting.

Success!

To me the Work is termed successful by the degree to which kindness, generosity, and compassion are embodied here and now, and not only embodied obviously but expressed in all areas of ordinary land extraordinary life (after all even the most exalted mystical states are not exempt from the Law, which in this case is the ongoing animation of the aforementioned qualities). No amount of destined or predicted greatness, no Divine Karma takes the place of the physical expressions of care and "mothering" of all sentient creatures.

What to Give Up to the Work

We can be very generous with our talent and creativity and decency. We go into old-age homes and homes for the emotionally disturbed and take care of them with great compassion, and this is all well and good. We're very generous with those things, but it's the things that we hold onto *until death do us part* that really have value to the Work. Our pride, vanity, guilt, greed—those are gold to the Work. If we're willing to offer up those things, to function as adults, free of the chokehold of personality and psychology—in other words, *ego*—then we interest the Work.

Respect the Teaching

What the master wants of the disciple is that the disciple be themselves completely. There is external, formal respect, but what really demonstrates respect is to embody the teaching. In the West we are hard and cynical, and on the other hand, we are very gullible. If we look at any major social phenomena, how people blindly follow musicians or movie stars, for example, those kinds of things are buffers from Reality.

Interiorly, the sign of respect for the teaching is practice, because no matter how sincere you are, the road to hell is paved with good intentions. It's wonderful to have good intentions, but good intentions are fickle, because the next day could be full of bad intentions. Respect means you take what it is you are respecting seriously enough to make it part of your life every day.

4 Cheers for Beauty

"... with beauty we conquer," wrote Nicholas Roerich. For what is it to "conquer" but to pierce the blindness of identification with thingness; to find ourselves drowned in the context of separation and have the life raft of beauty pull us out of the ocean of sloth and delusion. With beauty we conquer, we transcend the dualities of this and that, good and bad, one and two, nothing and everything, today, yesterday and tomorrow, desire and dullness, pity and sentiment. All right, three cheers, *oh hell, let's make it four,* for beauty!

Accept What God Provides

———

It is surely not necessary to avoid samadhis and blisses. Simply do not over-evaluate them, or see them in ignorance of their true and appropriate place in the scheme of things. Enjoy what is given and, in the context of a lifetime of Work and Devotion, accept what God provides with reverence and gratitude. Whether you receive a yacht or a pencil as a gift, you are still basically the same person. Whether a devotee receives a month of mindless God communion, or a second of visionary dreams, he or she is still basically the same devotee. The important rule of spiritual life is to continue to do the Work, under all conditions and circumstances, not allowing special surprises and unexpected revelations to make one feel "special," or an exception, nor to distract from the discipline and eternality of one's spiritual practices and true relationality.

"Lay Down Your Weapons" – A Song Lyric

lay down your weapons,
your swords and your guns,
lay down your sharp words
the bigotry and puns.
pick up one or two things
like kindness and like peace
and pass them out to everyone
the gentle and the beasts

violence only brings on
violence in its turn
fire only brings on
just a harsher burn
aggression ain't the answer
to the struggles of this life
no matter how we want it
it only creates strife

Antidote

The antidote to cynicism is faith.

Basic Meditation Practice, Part II

If you're actually paying attention during meditation, you will begin to notice a commonality to all experience. Ordinarily you go, "Oh, my mind is obsessing about sexual fantasies and that's not meditation. I should be thinking about something spiritual." But if we're really paying attention, we start to notice that there's a common thread to everything that arises, whether it's a physical feeling, a thought, an emotion, a fantasy, or a deep profound consideration of some sacred subject matter. And once we start to notice that thread of commonality, we start to follow the thread naturally—not by an effort of will, but we naturally find ourselves coming back to the thread, following that thread of commonality. And that thread of commonality begins to lead us to a space that is prior to whatever experience we're having, or we could say *deeper* than whatever experience we're observing, and then we start to get more to the actual essence of meditation.

"Neti Neti" and Enquiry

———

Whenever we fixate on something specific as *what is*, then we exclude everything else, and that is false. With the use of the phrase *neti neti* [not this, not this] we notice whatever arises in consciousness and say, "Reality is not this." If we say *neti neti* about everything—our projections on our children, our mates, all of it—until we get to the base of reality, which is *what is, here and now,* eventually we stop focusing on specifics and functioning in a dualistic way and come to the essential. We stop separating reality; we accept it as it is in its totality.

Enquiry is very similar. We Enquire of every emotion, feeling, thought, saying, "Who am I kidding?" That phrase is like a sword that cuts through every illusion until no illusion can stand in the face of it and nothing is left but the Source of Creation—what is.

The Truth Is an Act of Rebellion

Who are those who are most successful on the Path? Those who are most rebellious! To say yes to life, to accept what is as it is, in principle sounds very common sense, ordinary and obvious. But in fact to actually live that truth is an act of rebellion because you have to revolt against everything that defines you and controls you and implicates you in your psychological and egoic dynamics. Only a radical break with what we imagine reality to be can give us a glimpse of what Reality *is*.

The Test of Practice

———

Can we practice under any circumstance? Can we practice in the hospital room when our mother is dying? Can we practice when our teenage son gets into trouble? This is the ongoing process of the Path, of the Work. As we continue to live, life continues to produce circumstances that are unique and new in our experience, and we keep getting opportunities to apply our clarity. The test of practice is not, "I've realized this condition of enlightenment." The test of practice is, "Great! You've realized enlightenment. Okay, how are you going to live from now on?" Is your day-by-day life one of forgiveness, of compassion, of understanding, of service?

About Responsibility

It requires the same degree of discipline to keep small responsibilities as large ones. In the world of illusion, some big responsibilities require greater skill, more time or effort, and yet in the karmic world, to fall short of a small responsibility carries the same consequence as to fall short of a large responsibility. I will often give a student a task, one that not only can I do much better, but which I would much prefer to do myself, and yet it is so dynamically important for people to be able to responsibly carry some discipline into service— service which they not only want and appreciate but even crave—that I'd rather sacrifice my own comfort or preference in order to allow someone else the chance to bring consistency and devotion into their wish to serve.

So, please take your responsibilities seriously, whatever they are—be they bringing a glass of water at a regular time, or managing an orphanage of 200 children. Bringing the glass of water could have a greater "payoff" than managing the orphanage properly.

Living Alone

To be able to manage your attention you must be willing to live alone. Not that you will necessarily end up doing so, but if you are not willing to, it will be impossible to control your attention, to place it in its home—its right place. There must be no limits, no expectations, and no fixated or narrow ideas of what this management of attention will produce. Otherwise, you will be continually fascinated and seduced, and you'll have no ability to resist the attraction of those things that promise you the fulfillment of your desires (which to ego means Heaven) or the nonfulfillment of your fears or resistances. Every shaman is willing to live alone. Most rarely ever do, but they are willing to.

A Secure Home

Children who are not wounded learn quickly. If they are wounded, they keep putting themselves in situations to reinforce the wound. Have faith in your kids' innate essence. Make their situation at home as secure as possible, and they will learn. Be generous. When children grow up, what they remember is their parents' generosity.

No Inherent Value

———

There is no more inherent value to suffering than to beauty. If we make use of suffering, then it has value to the Path; it's the same thing with beauty in all its forms, living and not living. For example, just having a child does not mean that we learn anything at all—we have to make use of the situation. If not, they don't. Similarly, the common belief in some spiritual systems is that suffering is good. Like the Christian penitents: people gave themselves pain because they believed that God wanted them to suffer. I've never been able to support that philosophy—*and*, suffering arises, in the body, in the mind, in the world. When we intersect with suffering, whether we make it useful or not depends on the strength of our practice.

Working with the Essential Cramp

Start with training attention which will show you how often you are not resting in the disposition prior to anger or fear—attention about how you use your mouth with what you say to whom, how you say it, the tone in your voice, how often you say it. Begin to observe objectively, dispassionately, without drawing conclusions.

To fully rest in the context of freedom, however, there is no "how to" that applies. A free disposition is not something you attain, reach through effort, or master through work or apprenticeship. Rather, it's a matter of relaxing into, not growing into something. It's a question of distillation and refinement. What is left after distilling and distilling and distilling is Context, the essence of all this.

Putting the Cart before the Horse

Sex education from my viewpoint is essentially about working with denial, confusion, unconsciousness, the cramp, recoil, reactivity—whatever you call it. If you clear up the obstacles in that domain, you don't need sex education. The essential urge to join in communion and travel through the labyrinth of love between man and woman is completely instinctual. It needs no training. Man and woman, as polarities in the great universal scheme of things, actually know the way through that labyrinth. You will know the way when nothing stands in between your knowledge (which I refer to as Organic Innocence), and your journeying. All the things that do stand in between are the things that you need to work on.

So, to train yourself in esoteric sexual techniques, in the manipulation of body systems, is putting the cart before the horse.

The Coverup and the Cross

A sign on the board of a fundamentalist Christian church in Texas: "The cross won't cover what we won't uncover." Right on, Reverend! God's Blessings don't absolve us of our ignorance, or in other words Grace is not the answer to the dispelling of the lie, it is the revealing, the exposure of the lie that finally opens us to the possibility of Graceful Activity or Transformation. Even the power or force of Blessings can't pierce the armor of our denial. As long as we do not in any way begin to allow a glimmer of the perception of what comprehensive illusion we are under to send the rays of the Light of God and Truth into our locked down prison of falsehood, all of our "prayers" and pleas, of our so-called faith, of our passionate beliefs and impassioned assertions of reality (*our* reality) are to no avail. We will continue to suffer, to stew in the toxic juices of our own blindness. We must *uncover* what we have covered up all our lives, *we* must do this work, the "cross" won't do it for us and the "cross" won't make it all good.

The Real Hero

———

The hero is the one who will, not necessarily unflinchingly, confront head on the false premises—both the contextual false premise: the assumption of separation, the identification with the trappings of the illusion of substantiality, permanence and discrete individuality; and the relative false premises: our cultural and even biological conditioning, the imprints of our environment, family, media and the whole extended agreement of the lie, the refusal to "accept what is, as it is, here and now." The hero is the one who understands that no effort is wasted, that no practice is useless, that no sincere investigation, no intention and no attention goes unnoticed (by the Universe, Life—God, if you will), and based on that moves forward, charges into "battle," or slowly creeps on, plugging away with fortitude and stick-to-itiveness, even if impatient, doubtful or pessimistic, commits to practice and obeys that commitment with integrity, even if enthusiasm in every moment is too much to ask. The hero is the one who survives when others have dropped out, given up or turned on the teacher and teaching. The hero persists and actively engages the teaching and the practice, willing to deal with themselves, on all levels and unwilling to settle for mediocrity, in practice or in life.

Not Following the Recipe

A recipe is just like an outline and it can be adjusted. If you can't adjust a cooking recipe you sure as hell won't be willing to adjust your life recipe, which is no more than an outline as well, and no more to be taken completely dogmatically than a cooking recipe.

You all know for a fact that there are many people who can't (not *will not*, but *cannot*) *not* follow a recipe exactly, to the letter, as if the recipe-SWAT-team would immediately crash through the kitchen roof or window the instant they used maple syrup instead of the white sugar the recipe called for, putting a gun to their head and shouting: "DROP THE MAPLE SYRUP. NOW."

All recipes are meant to be frameworks within which a grown-up mature adult, and many times children as well, will use their sense of the vast possibility of the Universe, detailed in the specific sphere of time and place and circumstance of the moment, to make adjustments to suit the "chamber-du-jour."

162

Our Preoccupation

———

We are often willing to stick to confusion as our occupation and make it a habitual pattern of everyday life. In fact, that seems to be one of the main occupations of ego. Confusion provides a stable, familiar ground to sink into. It also provides a tremendous way of occupying ourselves. That seems to be one of the reasons there is a continual fear of giving up or surrendering. Stepping into the open space of the meditative state of mind seems very irritating to us, because we are quite uncertain about how to handle that wakeful state. Therefore, we would rather run back to our own cell than be released from prison.

Genuine Sorrow

Sorrow is not the root of anger, but anger masks sorrow. If anger were not used as a distraction, sorrow would naturally arise, and this sorrow would be greatly humbling and awesomely transforming. This genuine sorrow is grief for the human condition: recognizing the impossibility of perfection in relation to God, seeing ourselves as who we really are, stripped of our ego pretenses and free of our projections, wishes, hopes and fears. To live on the basis of *this Reality* would be so freeing and life-confirming that nothing else would be desired.

Fear and Anger

Don't delude yourself or compromise your own ability to be freely happy by making the false assumption that the things or circumstances in your life are the reasons for either happiness or its opposites. Those circumstances are superficial explanations. They have nothing to do with the essential dispositions of anger or fear that you function with, defend yourself against, and express yourself with. Enquire about those.

Death and Denial

———

Death, and everything it is associated with, is still too scary for most people to deal with directly. Too bad. Until we, each of us, deal with death, straight ahead and free from illusion, projection, fear of loss and doubt, we will be quite stymied in our attempts to fully profit from the Path. I'm not suggesting we begin to unemotionally slay small animals as a way to confront our denial, and at the same time it is useful, particularly useful, to not avoid the reality that we are, without question, mortal. And all lurid tales of ageless yogis living forever in youthful bodies, impervious to time, aging and disintegration, are worth just so many 3-dollar bills. 'Cause you, yes you, are gonna age, deteriorate, and ultimately, maybe a lot sooner than you expect or wish, drop that thing for a more subtle existence. Ain't no use pretending otherwise, especially as those beautiful wrinkles give your face more character. Dying can be a bit trying, yes, but death is no biggie. Death is always here, somebody is always dying.

The Trap of "I'm Sorry"

"I'm sorry." Too many people apologize too often for too many things for too many wrong reasons. It's just a function of immaturity and insecurity. We have so much trouble, in our mad, mad world, growing up and being moderately sane. And, it is still possible to notice our annoying affectation ("I'm sorry, I'm sorry") and not respond to the impulse, to the itch. Back to self-observation I'm afraid. If only we could do this Work and avoid ourselves, avoid self-honesty, avoid "accepting what is, as it is, here and now," yes if only we could, life would be so lovely, so easeful, so, well, unconscious, wouldn't it? But we can't, sorry. Really, I'm sorry. It isn't my fault but that doesn't matter at all, I'm still sorry. Sorry.

Cream Rises to the Top

———

This is the Work, man! The work is a mill and you are the wheat. Does the mill say "Thank you" to every grain of wheat that it grinds, that it pulverizes into dust? No. This is the Work. We have a lot of fun, we get together and laugh and have great food, great music. And the sangha is fabulous. When you bond in, this is what you've always wanted. But don't kid yourself. Out of four liters of milk in one container, how much cream is on the top? Every atom of milk in that bottle loves every other atom of milk, but there ain't that much cream on the top. You all know the difference in taste between cream and milk, and so does God, so don't fool yourself. When it comes right down to the bottom line, God is a jealous lover, and if you don't want to work, somebody else will. The line of loose women waiting to get a shot at the Beloved is so long you can't even see the end of it! I'm not talking in terms of gender. I mean women *and men* who want to be in the Work.

The Need for Solitude

Everyone, at some phase of sadhana, needs some time alone. Not alone with new companionship or necessarily with new environments. But truly alone, in the monastic sense. There comes a point in the "completion" of the communication of the Lord—from the fantastic, or the magical, to the ordinary, functional, pragmatic movement in the world—when the one "being completed" simply needs a temporary period of solitude. This should not be mistaken by the immature student whose tendencies are separative and selfish to mean that regular and constant "aloneness" is an appropriate aspect of initial and basic Godlife. One must be quite mature before this phase of solitude can be real and true.

The Stupidity of Denial

Our underworld—what is "covered," our "sins"—are not made clean, in some wishful or hopeful way, as long as we stay in firm denial and fail to give God, or whatever you wish to call it, Life, Reality, Truth, just due (i.e., fail to "accept what is, as it is, here and now"). So, we have to dig, in a sense, to unearth that which is covered by our refusal to see in an Objective way, our refusal to be ruthlessly self-honest. To sit around, unwilling to practice, unwilling to self-observe (without judgment, which is one of the criteria that defines self-observation, over and against some superficial noticing and judgmental interpretation of random manifestations), unwilling to surrender, unwilling to serve the other in our narcissism, unwilling to make effort, and assume that the Divine Influence of the Guru and Lineage, or the Love of Jesus Christ, will "save" us, regardless of how ugly our behavior is, how selfish we are, or vain, or prideful, violent or lying and cheating, how lacking in empathy, compassion and generosity or kindness we may be, is just rank stupidity.

Humility

———

Humility is one of the rarest human qualities. A lot of people who are personally insecure and full of self-hatred might always put themselves second, but that is not humility, that is psychological debasement. Humility is the capacity to be genuinely full of awe in the face of the majesty of Reality, instead of thinking that we are intelligent and powerful enough to actually run the world—for example, by playing around with genetics and controlling nuclear fission, which obviously gets out of control.

All for You

Practice is for *you*. What's important is that *you* know that you are practicing with integrity—even though nobody else knows; even if you could fool everybody, and nobody would ever find out. What matters is that *you know* you have integrity.

Like a Little Child

Maturity is a matter of "becoming like a little child," with the clear, intelligent revelation of adult consciousness and intention. The purposeful and responsible acceptance of God's Gift, and movement with intention and pleasure as God's Will, is the sign of maturity. The infant does all of this spontaneously and naturally, because it's the only thing to do! All other so-called signs of adulthood—the jaded education of scholars, the hot air of praise and braggadocio, the macho stance of the insecure man and the liberated feminist—all are just delusions of grandeur and in fact gross immaturity. To become as a child with adult realization of and reliance on God is true maturity, and the only possible (and viable) alternative to a life of pain, suffering, and interminable unhappiness.

Losing the Body

To lose the body is to gain the body. Really. It's a paradoxical statement, but it's true. When you "realize" the body, you realize some kind of detachment: "This is just the body, it doesn't define me. I'm associated with it, and in my association I am the body, and when the body leaves I will still be." When you have realized the context of "being one with" [in the teaching of Swami Prajnanpad] the body, then the body is not a burden. It's not extra. It's not something you have to carry around, an annoyance. It's just what it is. You know, when the body is hungry, it's hungry. When it's tired, it's tired. It's just what it is. Looking at the body as some kind of cross you have to bear is not having realized, or not having seen clearly, that it is just a body—no more, no less.

November 17, 1994
(for Yogi Ramsuratkumar)

———

I don't need hashish —
    I smoke my Father's Rags,
and stagger off
    lost to all but He.
I am drunk —
    blind and deaf
to the pleas
    of the sober.

Put Mind in Its Place

———

When your mind is plaguing you—with jealousy or whatever—say, "Shut the fuck up! I have work to do!" Put your mind in its place. "You aren't God—you're just the mind! Get off your throne!" Not, "Yes, mind, how long shall I be confused, mind? Suffer? For years?" When we're not being pushed around by mind, genuine acceptance can arise, giving us the possibility to live with clarity instead of being crushed by circumstances.

Rest in the Obvious

———

We can be present to what is objectively obvious without having to figure anything out about it. Much of what we call the Blessing Force of Yogi Ramsuratkumar and the lineage, or loosely call "Grace," works in this way: one day we simply show up altered, different. I never recommend questioning such wonderful gifts, but I do recommend simply accepting "what is" with gratitude and wonder. To dig around—or more accurately to root around like a pig looking for slop—when such investigations are no more than the perverse wishes to "understand" something, often just creates a big mud hole. It would do us all well to learn to rest in what is objectively obvious (not what is obvious to an ego full of biases, confusion, misinterpretations and false identifications).

Trusting Yourself

To trust yourself does not mean you'll never make a mistake; it means that whatever circumstances you find yourself in, you'll make use of the situation. Whether you make good or bad decisions, to trust yourself is to trust your practice and commitment to the Path. When your practice is stable and a state of presence is known and established, dignity and nobility will shine through you.

Becoming Accident Prone

We have to practice rigorously, even though practice does not linearly lead to realization. It has been said that enlightenment is an accident, and practice makes us accident-prone. Practice establishes an environment that encourages maturity, clarity, and breakthrough. It doesn't guarantee it, but it makes it more likely.

Luxury Reactivity

At a certain level of maturity, reactivity is a luxury you can ill afford. Reactivity then becomes a sickness. You need to seriously consider that reactivity to anything that arises in this Work is a luxury. The more mature you become in this Work, the poorer you become. One would think you would become richer as you progress, but you don't. You become poor in spirit, as the man said.

Bliss Is Not Boring

Generally, we get happy and want more, get sad and want less. But the practice is to "become one with" [Swami Prajnanpad] *whatever* is. And to "become one with" gives everything the same flavor: *ananda*. One reason people don't pursue that practice is we assume that if everything is equal there will be no texture, and that is a wrong assumption. We assume if we're not identified with anything, it will become bland, like perfectly creamed mashed potatoes! But, *ananda* is infinitely textured.

"Hard to Work With"

If you want to live peacefully, it behooves you to remember that the other person is never at fault for your emotional reactivity. The problems arise when we react to others as if our reactions were justified and the other person's behavior is somehow wrong, unjust, detrimental and aggressive.

There are people who have a big reputation for being difficult to work with. They are demanding, impatient, impossible to please, easily irritated and angered, unjust in their demands—that doesn't make them hard to work with. Why they have this reputation is because the people who work with them refuse to accept them as they are, refuse to see their behavior as not only completely mechanical, but that they're suffering far more than the one who is reacting. It is our reaction that creates our pain, our own suffering, not the behavior of those we react to and recoil from.

Reasonableness

———

The single significant ingredient that keeps us from celebrating our lives together in true worship of the Divine is our reasonableness. Our attempt to make sense of things or find reason in things devastates our spontaneity and innocence.

Passion for the Teaching

My friends, it is all about the Teaching—not just learning it in our heads, which most of us do quite well, but embodying it so the practice is the first thing to arise inwardly and outwardly, in thought, feeling and action, in every moment, prior to the lightning-speed reaction of the psychological script. That is our Work. In order for that to come to pass, we cannot afford to be lazy, laid back or lacking in passion about, around, and for this Teaching. We must constantly be studying, in the context of the Teaching, using every life situation and circumstance to reflect back to us directly in relation to the Teaching, always self-observing, considering, looking for that opportunity, that possibility for Work, for breakthrough, for transformation, to be given a task, for another piece of the puzzle that is our labyrinth, both the labyrinth of the dream, the lie of illusion, and the labyrinth of Truth, the Real, of Being. There is no time to rest, except in the obvious ways that conserve energy and keep us healthy and sharp so we can actually be passionate instead of exhausted and worn out.

Sacred Marriage

———

Sacred marriage means to create an overall environment of sanctuary for one another's spiritual work or practice. You free your partner to do the spiritual work he or she needs to do, while you also provide your absolute support. And all this is done within the context of intimacy, tenderness, and sexual communion. Sacred marriage frees the partners, rather than controls them. Marriage, in a sense, is vowing that you will never complicate your mate's sadhana with envy, pettiness, competition, or greed.

Enlightened Community

Devote your life to enlightened community, not enlightenment. The reason for "my" problems is that we really believe, on some primal level, that we are separate from God and we see ourselves as isolated, independent events in the universe. If we realized that community is the essential manifestation of the Great Process of Divine Evolution, and that selflessness establishes the height of ecstasy—that you are happiest, genuinely happiest when you have the least concern for your own personal isolation—why would anyone not work toward making that a viable possibility?

Blindness to Contradictions

———

A discussion arose about the two polarities of devotion and the ordinary activities of life. It arose relative to a car that pulled into the parking lot of Starbucks. The car haphazardly and too quickly pulled into a "handicapped only" space, and two women practically leapt out and strode, quite unhandicappedly, into our very Starbucks, which is when I read the saying on the front bumper that stated, "With God all things are possible."

I regaled my associates there and then with my bon mot, which was, "All things are possible except parking properly in an appropriate space," or to put it another way, "Yes, all things are possible, even parking in a handicapped space and a foot over the line at that." And then, ever the lacking-in-compassion-for-idiot-drivers guru, I said: "Hypocrites." All of which led to a discussion of faith, dedication, love, devotion and all of that, and how we can be filled with genuine qualities such as those and yet still be either blind to our contradictory behaviors or really have no clue as to the immaturity of our psychological complexes and their effect on others and on our world.

On the Spot

When you are looking for an answer to a question, relax the rigidity of your attitudes and expectations, because the answer comes through circumstance: something happens, or we find ourselves with a certain opportunity or lack of opportunity. Because we have a fixated and rigid idea, we don't recognize the answer. Cultivate a mood of just seeing what shows up; be prepared to check out what shows up right there on the spot, when it shows up. Chögyam Trungpa Rinpoche called this "on-the-spot-ness." Cultivate an attitude of openness and possibility so that you can see what happens in the next moment, because with professional work, relationships, and many things, our greatest life opportunities come when we least expect them and from the least expected place.

Time to Earn Merit

———

I do wish more of us would open our eyes, truly, and open our hands in kindness and generosity "above and beyond the call of ego." Go on. Earn some merit now. Don't wait until you have some time on your hands. Time is willing to be "made," so make it. Make the time and get on out there and earn that merit. In fact, junior and senior merit earners, don't just put your toes in the water, go to town, and paint it golden and azure, forest green and violet. On the count of three: one, two, three: CHARGE.

The Next Step

When we start to recognize that the little choices we make during the day are completely conditioned by something in our unconscious, it stimulates an even deeper investigation. One of the most useful pieces of information about transformation or self-knowledge is that, metaphorically speaking, there are a series of doors and rooms. You can't start in the last room; you have to start at the first room, then go into the second, the third and the fourth. Every door is locked. Every room is locked. The only key we have is the key to the first room, then the key to each consecutive room is in the previous room. So, we open the first room because we have the key, and the key to the second room is in the first room, and so on. If we are willing to look for the key in the room we're in, we'll find it. Sometimes it's obvious, and sometimes it's hidden away, but the key to the next room is always in the room that we're in. We don't need a whole program. All we need is the next step, and if we take that step, within the taking of that step is the key to the next step.

Not Happy

———

My idea of being happy? Let me tell you what it *is not*. It's not being so committed to the Work, whatever the hell that is, that everybody in the environment is miserable as a result of your intensity. You're not supposed to plod through life gnashing your teeth. The Work isn't supposed to be *work*. It's supposed to be Suffering, not suffering.

"Everybody" – A Song Lyric

Everybody's right, everybody's wrong
Everybody's weak, everybody's strong
Everybody's left, everybody's right
Everybody's lonely in the middle of the night
Everybody's good, everybody's bad
Everybody's happy, everybody's sad
Everybody's soft, everybody's hard
We all got weeds growin in the yard
Everybody's one, everybody's two
Everybody's old, everybody's new
Everybody's ugly, everybody's fine
We're all drunk on the same wine
Everybody's bitter, everybody's sweet
Everybody's messy, everybody's neat
Everybody's young and everybody's old
Everybody's everybody if the truth be told

The Aim of Conscious Childraising

The idea is for a child to grow up knowing, tacitly and organically, beyond any doubt and confusion, that they are loved absolutely, for who they are, without the demand for any particular performance, manifestation, achievement, or drama.

How Emptiness Gets Filled

———

Give the Beloved an inch and He'll (She'll?) take the mile. Don't make it a business deal, full of mutual reward and expectation. Give the Beloved an inch completely free of contractual obligation and the Beloved will pick up speed—cautiously at first, we being the sneaky, sophisticated ego-beings that we are—but finding you Faithful in your resolve and in your Adoration and free as well of wants and supplication, the Beloved will fill the emptiness with Itself and all that implies.

All Is Transitory

You are afraid that the "big one," the moment of release, will be just as transitory as your Christmas toys. And it is. For enlightenment is the knowledge that all experience is transitory, including enlightenment. That is not an indictment of experience; the Lord delights in the transitory, it is the humor of God.

With Presence, There Is Choice

To "become one with" [Swami Prajnanpad] anger, violence, or aggression is to find yourself in a state of presence in which you are noticing what is arising, and noticing it is not you—which gives you a choice. Like getting on a ride at Disneyland. Obviously the ride is not you. If it looks attractive, you take it. If it doesn't look attractive, you don't take it. You are not obligated to get on the ride; you are not obligated to any anger, violence or any form of ignorance and suffering. From presence, there is choice: from ego, only relative choice. You can say, "Yes, this is arising"; not my anger—just, anger is arising. Unconditionally accept and you will notice something curious—the doorway is open, but you aren't jumping through the door.

A Call to Action

———

I cannot remain untouched and untroubled, and in this state of trouble and touchedness I must complain and address the inequities and sins of those who refuse to be Blessed by the breath and caress of the Divine in Its personal and Transcendent Forms. To deny the Reality of Transformation and to allow ego and all its criminal animations to run unchecked over every Sacred ideal, over every objective Good is, as far as I am concerned, demanding condemnation and much, much more than that, demanding action in the contrary camp, action that establishes the "Kingdom of God" on earth and in the heart and soul of Mankind. Nothing less will satisfy me, and nothing less should satisfy you either.

Ease Up on Ego

The process of any true form of spiritual life is not to get rid of ego. It is, after all, an integral part of your existence. Did you ever see a human being function without ego? The error lies in ego's pretensions to be absolute, to being separate unto itself. The attempt to kill it gives substance to these pretensions and implies that it has an independent life that must be destroyed. The process is to accept it, enjoy it, and observe it with humor. When your ego surfaces and you know that something is ego-motivated, be responsible for that and enjoy it. The process is Grace, not struggle.

The Process Is Feminine

Transformation is not a masculine process. The "Work" is not a masculine process. Practice, Sadhana, Surrender to the Will of God are not masculine processes. Many people assume they need to batter practice, to club it to death until finally they will dominate, win, end up victorious. But this approach does not work, plainly and simply.

The process is feminine and the keys to the lock which imprisons Reality or Truth is in a feminine approach. We must go at this knot of confusion, called the mind or sleep or unconsciousness or illusion or maya, with very gentle, humorous, patient, accepting relationships to it. We can practice vigorously but with bright and flexible vigor, not rigid, righteous vigor. We must give ourselves time to relax into this Enlightenment, whatever it is, rather than trying to force it to take us over, permeate our fears and illusion (which of course it cannot do). If we approach the Work as Woman, we may just discover something quite unexpected and surprising, but no less delightful.

As We Progress

When we enter the Path, we do not see things clearly; we are not very sensitive. As we grow and as our work deepens, the veils of illusion dissipate that were keeping us asleep. It doesn't mean that things have become worse since we started to work on ourselves, but that we are taking the buffers away and that we are suddenly more sensitive than we have ever been before. We actually are making less mistakes than before, but we are more disturbed by our mistakes because we see their implications more clearly. We absolutely cannot avoid this reaction: we cannot be blind and see at the same time. The process has to do with always seeing more deeply and more clearly—seeing everything.

Christmas Day, 1988
(for Yogi Ramsuratkumar)

———

Oh! My Father,
Yogi Ramsuratkumar:
I came to You hungry
and You fed Your son such a satisfying meal.
You sly Beggar, You —
How was I to know
that to be fed by my Father
would increase the hunger
         a hundredfold?

The Assumption of Scarcity

We assume that everything in life is scarce. No mental dialogue takes place relative to an "idea" of scarcity. We don't learn it objectively in school, yet we are taught it as sure as we breathe. We learn it right down to our cells. We assume that everything in life is scarce, especially those things of some spiritual value: security, love, friendship, and consideration. We primally feel we must personally control and manage everything and everyone in order not to "lose" their benefits or attention. We think: "I'll never have enough, so I better protect, secure, assure what I have so it can't be lost, stolen, or run away on its own."

No Grand Gestures

———

Everything starts with self-observation. You don't have to make gigantic gestures. You can do small things: the way you shift your gaze, the way you put your mind into a different thinking pattern, the way you hold your fork differently. Very small things have gigantic repercussions. You don't have to be some kind of hero; you don't have to climb Mount Everest: "Okay, I'm going to confront my fear!" You can just make small gestures. If you're afraid of snakes, how do you confront your fear? You do not say, "Okay, I'm afraid of snakes, so I'm going to milk the poison out of cobras!" You go to a reptile zoo and find someone who's trained and knows snakes and will help you play for a few minutes with a snake that is not poisonous and will not bite.

Take the Plunge

From a place of burden, weight and clutter, you can't appreciate the spacious unclutter, the lightness of being. You can only know it from its actual presence—that is, after you take the plunge. You can't know what a mango tastes like from a picture of it, or from someone else's ecstatic description; you have to taste it. You can't know how cold the water is until you jump off the bank, and that's the only way to do it—jump, not put in one toe to test it out.

Do it or not, but not doing is to remain in ignorance, left to your habits and your insecurities. And doing it, remember there is no formula, no method, no magic wand or magic pill. Simply put down the mass of mess and walk away.

Thou Art That

———

It is common for spiritual students to dwell on their personal problems for long periods of time before coming to realize that an individual's "own" neuroses are almost irrelevant in the scheme of things. The personal or isolated vision of ourselves as fragmented beings, separate from God and striving in individual ways to return to some kind of nebulous union with this God of our dreams, is a complete fallacy. We are already, always united, or more correctly, we are always already that which we think we must seek for.

Dangerous Expectations

There are stories of wonderful deaths, of miraculous deaths, and I wonder if these could actually be a handicap. This kind of story can either be very inspiring or very dangerous if people start to think that that is what they want for themselves. It is much more useful to see that everything is impermanent, that the body will die no matter what, and that there will be a much more important transition than having a few wrinkles and a few grey hairs.

Authenticity

———

It's really difficult to have dignity, maybe even impossible, if *you* are not authentic. I suppose one could be completely authentic about one's inauthenticity, but I only suppose it because I can't see that it would be really possible. Authenticity in all things— art, relationship (which doesn't mean to say everything that comes to one's feeble and inflated mind), use of money and other resources, social concerns, professional function—may not always be the popular choice, but it is the only right choice. Authenticity, by the way, does not mean that you need to "cut off your nose to spite your face" in the name of patriotism or honesty. You could lie through your teeth if it didn't hurt anyone, or do great damage, or if it was to protect you, your family, your village or your environment from the ravages and profiteering of a world gone mad.

The Small Stuff

———

Somebody once said, "God is in the details." I don't believe that. My philosophy is: "Don't sweat the small stuff." If you think most things through, you really don't have to address the small stuff. The worst thing that can happen is that the soup is too salty, or the meal isn't so good.

Don't Trust Ego

———

We're not trustworthy in our egos. Look how many people spend a lifetime in ethical service and then crumble in a certain circumstance. Until the moment we die, ego is not trustworthy. Don't trust your ego—trust your *self*.

Try This Experiment

So… to the experiment, which you are free to try or not, as you wish. Try to "assume" love, to assume that it *is,* already present, given, already accessible, without compromise or limit. That is simply it. "Assume" love. To "assume" in this way is to tacitly realize, to accept absolutely, positively, without question or thought, without reflection or distinction. The statement is: love is.

Any hint, even the slightest breeze, of territoriality, of possessiveness, of greed in relationship to love will send it running for cover. So, the assumption is a radical one, as in "love *is,*" here, now, already true, already ready, rather than "love is not" and therefore needs to be found, discovered and, the ego says, imprisoned so that it cannot escape. There is no substitute for Reality. There is no alternative to Reality. There are no options to Reality. And the Reality is: love is. The more we "assume" this Reality, the more likely that this Reality will assume us. Try it, the odds are small but there are odds; lean on it and stay leaned on it, the odds increase; Realize Reality, all bets are off. Thank you.

Responsibility for Children

The responsibility of being with children—either in an official capacity as a teacher or parent, or simply as a friend or companion—is literally a responsibility for the future of humankind. What we model for children, how we treat them, how we parent them, is more than important—it is absolutely vital to their mental, emotional and physical health and well being and to that of the earth itself.

An Invitation

—◆—

May the heat of suffering
Become the fire of love.

Keeping Things to Scale

Our own identification with the willing victim "I" creates furor over insignificance. Why be a victim of the victim? With a modicum of awareness, you won't be so easily trapped in such grossly obvious situations. If you simply try, try, and keep on trying, and if your efforts are sincere and not motivated to make points with the authority, be it the Guru or God, you will inevitably build Work success and find those attempts rewarded, and quite richly I will add. So if you must react or recoil, at least keep the scale commensurate to the actual provocation, and please do try to pause for a moment and think before you blurt out or do something truly vile, for which you will be very sorry for a very long time.

Hope Springs Eternal

———

The great ideal of suffering is hope. Hope keeps one searching, because one is continually trying to change things into what one hopes it will be like someday. It keeps one focused on what "should be" and totally ignorant of what is. Hope is the expression of despair. I find it odd that people who say, "There is no hope," are always frowning. That news is cause for celebration.

Putting Ego In Its Place?

The ego doesn't need anything done *to* it. If one wants to begin to more dynamically and thoroughly manifest one's "intrinsic dignity, intrinsic nobility" [Swami Prajnanpad and Arnaud Desjardins], and the wisdom of true adult intelligence, all ego simply needs is to cognize itself and the laws of its own essential being exactly as it and they are. With this cognition, ego becomes a servant of the True Work instead of a dominant controller of the "Human Biological Machine" as Mr. E.J. Gold calls it (us).

The Myth of Separation

Try as we might, we can't *be* separate in any way from anyone or anything. Now that should be good news! In fact, in the Zen tradition, it is often told in stories that this simple revelation was enough for the struggling disciples to be "enlightened." And even though separation is only our fantasy of imagination relative to this issue, isn't it absolutely marvelous that we can get butter and cream from milk, and that our children move out of our house to lead their own lives at a certain point?

Listening Between the Lines

We need to hear one another, not just listen to the gross words that are spoken. We need to understand what the other is saying, reading not only between the lines, but deeply at the heart of any given matter. We need to hear and respond with sensitivity, tact, or diplomacy if necessary, with understanding, compassion, generosity, and certainly with patience and tolerance, not to mention spaciousness and a willingness to respond and serve as called for, even at the price of some personal discomfort or extra effort on our part. We need to "do unto others as we would wish others do unto us," which includes honoring and respecting their gross needs as well as their Work needs.

Yes and No

We remember ourselves every time we function intentionally in the relative world in a relative way. We can affirm, "This is not the ultimate practice, *and* this is what I'm doing right now, this is what I need to do right now." That act of awareness is, in fact, automatically and naturally drawing us toward the Absolute, because you cannot have one pole of a pair of opposites without the other. They both exist. When "yes" exists, then "no" exists. When light exists, darkness also exists. When the relative exists, the Absolute exists. When we consciously recognize the relative, we are also—perhaps unconsciously, but definitively—recognizing the Absolute in some way.

Building Conscious Love

———▼———

Conscious love does not occur by chance, but must be cultivated, engaged, activated and lived. People don't "fall" in conscious love. It comes from a tremendous amount of very hard work, one element being that you always need to observe yourself to determine whether what you want for your lover is what's best for him or her, or just your own egocentric preference.

"Building Love" will demand sacrifice and create heat, because every self-dramatizing and Divine-refusing bone in one's body (both physic and physical) will attempt to undermine and confuse the clarity and momentum one is developing in building and maintaining love. This process demands qualities that are extraordinary. But the result is also extraordinary in that it raises one from the gutter of ego to the position of a devotee of God.

At War with Illusion

Listen! I hope it becomes clear that we are at war: at war with sleep, with illusion, with the lie, the false. There can be no truce, no compromise, no pandering or catering to the enemy. There is only one winner: either Reality or Truth wins, or mechanicality and the psychological script wins. The enemy has no human feelings, no subtleties, no sensitivities; the enemy is pure survival, and this enemy takes no prisoners—it is all or nothing.

Yes, I know this sounds very dramatic! Without an absolute commitment to ruthless self-honesty, to objective clarity, and to realization of Truth (recognition, comprehension, integration or digestion and animation of Truth), to submission to the higher laws, to God, to the One, the Absolute, to Father in Heaven, one cannot wage war against an enemy that knows no ethic, has no rules except win at any cost, has no honor or regret. Please verify this through study of the great Realizers of any and all traditions.

Changing Others?

We can't force anybody else to be any other way than the way they are. We can provide education, we can make certain circumstances, provide opportunities, but we can't make anyone be other than they are. How they are is how they are. One of the mechanics of acceptance is recognizing this concept of personal integrity, because we can't define another person's reality. Nobody can. Jesus couldn't. Buddha couldn't. So, we certainly aren't going to. We can't accept what is as it is, here and now, if we're busy trying to force other people into our mold, even if it's a good mold of kindness and peace and so on.

Possibility Vs. Hope

When we are hoping for something, we're actually assuming that that thing is going to happen, and that assumption is a very effective obstacle to the thing actually happening. We're all human; we all have desires, wishes, hopes, dreams—even just for basic health and security. So it's a very delicate issue to hold the possibility of something without actually crossing the line of assuming that that possibility is already concretized. When we find ourselves hoping for something, there's nothing to do but just see that we're hoping for something and reestablish our intention to be in the present and hold possibility without weighing it down with our emotional desire. That's a matter of attention and practice and remembering this principle: when we have assumed something before that thing is concretized, that assumption usually dispels or minimizes the possibility of it happening.

Seek the Source

———

The teaching is like a spring: it arises from the depths of being and shows up ultimately on the surface, but the source of it is on the inside. When you don't have external support— like closeness to sangha on the Path, which is important and wonderful—it forces you to seek the heart of communion, which is not on the gross or dense physical level.

The Process of Surrender

Surrender may be associated with great difficulty, hard work, pain. With surrender one comes to feel a sharpened compassion for all beings, so one consequently feels more pain. There's just no way of getting around it. Yet, at the same time, it is never something that one would wish to be different. Surrendering is not dual. There is no "one" to wish that it could be different. The difficulty with surrender, from the dualistic perspective, is that surrender looks like extinction. Personality, which by its very nature is dualistic, thinks that to be nondualistic would mean being wiped out. It thinks that individuality, independence, one's uniqueness, would be wiped out, but really that's not true.

If one would just surrender, and stay in that state, one would realize that actually one is *more* of an individual, because all of a sudden you've got real options. Before surrender all of our options are absolutely defined by our survival strategy, and surrender doesn't look like a graceful, pleasant process to ego.

You Are Perfect

———

You are who you are—nothing adds or subtracts; that's reality. To choose who you are is bliss, *ananda*. That's the task. Who you are as you are is perfect—not in relation to good or bad, just perfect. That's where you need to be. Then all questions that arise from that which is heavily weighted, like having a child, to where to eat Thai food tonight—then all phenomena that arise become things you observe, you notice, and you see them as they are and make choices relative to them that are objective, not defined by ego, which is never neutral.

Doin' the Best Ya Can

There is no need to "get it perfect," the desire for which is mostly neurotic or misplaced anyhow (or anyway, if you prefer). What we're looking for is doing the best we can, under the circumstances and all things considered, like karmas, genetics, bioeverythings, the planets, and so on. At the same time, understand that we are looking for doing the best we can, not the best our psychological script tells us we can, not the best our friends, family, society, and culture tells us we can, not the best our wild subjectivity tells us we can, and not the best our mind-body limitations tells us we can. We are looking for doing the actual, Real, Objective, Divine best we can.

Cultivating Patience

Patience is a quality that can be cultivated, if it isn't something innate to us. When we superimpose our own subjective vision on any situation and are unable or unwilling to "accept what is, as it is, here and now," then we will inevitably be antsy when results don't meet our demanding, and often quite unrealistic, criteria, and our impatience is like pouring salt on a wound. I assume that most would like to be in life situations that, overall, were peaceful, delightful, productive, sensitive, elegant and dignified. Without patience, forbearance and acceptance of "what is, as it is, here and now," such a realization is highly unlikely. And since "patience begins at home," you must be patient with yourself, not overly critical when who you see yourself as does not match who you actually are now, as you are, all things considered. Patience, the acceptance of self, is immeasurably helpful in being able to apply such generosity of spirit and maturity of presence and action to others, eventually all others. This is the seed of true compassion: patience and acceptance, first in passive forms and then in more active forms, from benign patience to an actual reaching out.

A Tantric Path

Who we are first is human; that's our primal state of being, our blueprint, organically. Our potential as living beings is to be human. And then secondarily, within that context, there is man, woman, engineer, whatever we are, whoever we are, artist, teacher, nurse, therapist. This is what we've got to work with—our lives, as they are, our pleasures, our struggles, just as they are. The Hinayana Buddhist vehicle tells us to just notice it all and don't be attached to any of it, because it's all empty, all ultimately, essentially insubstantial. The Mahayana Buddhist vehicle says transcend it and then serve others who have not yet transcended it, and the Vajrayana vehicle says, here it is, let's do something with it. Anger—let's transform it into energy, vitality. Vanity—let's turn it into an appreciation of beauty. Fear—let's turn it into humility. Greed—let's turn it into generosity. That's my path.

Just Be Kind

You don't have to label your illusions to be able to live life in reality or truth. How you *act* is the first thing—that is, with kindness, generosity, compassion, dignity, respect, the ability to extract joy from life when there is joy, and sorrow from life when there is sorrow—regardless of what goes on internally. We can call that "discernment," or "discrimination."

Academically, if through your entire life you acted with impeccable integrity—serving others, and blessing the universe through the clarity of your behavior—it wouldn't matter *what* you were thinking or what you were doing interiorly. If you died having never indulged the negative obsessions of ego—the anger, the greed, the violence, the cruelty, the pettiness—then you would be considered a great saint (and probably you would be).

If we didn't "deal" with the mind at all, and simply *acted* in a way that was consistently reliable—with kindness, generosity, compassion, dignity, and so on—we might not *feel* enlightened, but we would *be* enlightened, at least as good as enlightened, and maybe even better.

The Purpose of the Path

Often we come to the Path and don't really want what the Path is; we just want to get rid of some bothersome aspect of our personality. Whatever gets us on the Path is fine, but sooner or later we have to understand that we haven't come to the Path to deal with the superficialities of personality and psychology. We may have to deal with these things secondarily in the process, but they are not the purpose of the Path. Becoming a good citizen is not the purpose of the Path. The purpose of the Path is to bring clarity to the illusion of separation. That's what the "No" is—that first psychological decision we make, in infancy, to view the world in separation. We don't know we're making the decision; we are not self-aware, but the decision still gets made and has its effects. So when we come to the Path as adults, the demand is simply to realize the reality of oneness—whether we language that demand as accepting what is as it is, here and now, or to saying "Yes to life."

The Value of Disturbance

———

Irritation is a valuable thing. If the oyster was never irritated, there would never be any pearl. If carbon atoms were never irritated, there would never be any diamonds and if certain molecular combinations were not irritated, we would not have nuclear power or intestinal gas. So irritation prevents you from being lazy and always procrastinating. It does not let you sleep, go from one day to the next saying, "Yes, everything is fine, no problem." It may not be very pleasant to be disturbed like this, but it is a great thing.

Freedom is the ultimate disturbance. You may think that if you become more successful on the Path, one day you will be free of all disturbances. But it is exactly the opposite. If you reach the ultimate goal in the Work, you will always be disturbed, but not by disturbances that arise in you. In the meantime, this irritation is one of the things that makes you go forward, forces you to go deeper and work more actively.

Avoid the Cultural Decline

Some of us have faced death and will never be the same, in a positive way. Others of us have faced death and are still the same, undoubtedly having made great resolutions before our recovery and then, safe and out of dangerous waters, have snapped back into the same primate sloth. This is a vigorous insult to this Path and this Work. We cannot afford such apathy. As our world at large slides into its own ugly sloth, its complete dumbing-down of decency, intelligence, common sense, even survival instincts except at the most violent levels, we cannot afford to be caught in this cultural decline. We must fight tooth and nail to rise to the demands of the triple gem—the Buddha, Dharma and Sangha—and to make a sanctuary of this rare, even precious, little flower we have begun to grow. Please, please, please.

Be Prepared Through Practice

The suffering in the world at large is not lessening in quantity or in intensity. I think that in our lifetime, the lie, the illusion, the massive darkness, and the illness of the refusal of Truth and Reality as-it-is will only grow more, as will people's general tendency to take it all hook, line and sinker. This suffering is highly likely to increase as people in general continue to be confronted by crisis, by strange behaviors as people go mad from tension and stress, from war, violence, senseless fundamentalism, political and corporate idiocy, greed and criminality, natural earth and sky upheavals, financial challenges, undiagnosable and virulent illness, all-around confusion, doubt, crises of faith and so on.

You will want to have your "practice shit" together. You will want to be stable and strong and clear in your intention, attention (and not addicted to e-tension), and able to pray profoundly for all that which you can't do anything about hands-on. Never mind being fearless; if you are, God bless your lucky ass! Mostly just be prepared to "do the right thing," fear be damned—and the torpedoes too, if necessary!

Know Less to Know the Real

You must be willing to know less. It is the nature of ego to bitch, to scream, and to put up defenses against knowing less and less. The key is the conscious and intelligent participation in the process of one's own undoing, so to speak. If there is a willingness to know less and less, then the process will work very gently. "More and more" is rational or logical justification for things that satisfy ego or mind. And "less and less" is what is necessary to be real. "More and more" is the need for proof. When you come to know nothing, you know everything. If you try to know everything, all you want is proof that you are "right," and then it is a hopeless case. Being willing to know less and less is being willing to get off it. To truly know one is no one, a hopeless fool, is often the epitome of a lifetime of spiritual practice.

Inner and Outer Spaces

If our outer world is cluttered, confused, dense and/or tense or full of stress, so too is our inner world. If our outer world is clean, precise, spacious and/or relaxed, so too is our inner world. Now the outer world can be sparse, even Zen-like in the actual content and still be cluttered, confused and so on. And the outer world, our outer world, can be quite full, rich with "things" and stimuli and still be clear, precise and so on. That is why *mood*, or as we are used to saying, *context* is the key element of this consideration.

We are always talking about "self-observation," as M. Gurdjieff considered it, and many people are, to be blunt, quite blind to their own manifestations, but our outer world is unmistakable and unmissable in its physical state. So, this can be a doorway into a more personal glimpse, or extended view even, *why not?*, of our bodily and emotional, even subtle manifestations. Our outer world is not a metaphor for anything, it is a literal extension, a duplicate Universe, if you will, that can be easily recognized and used to deepen this relevant, possibly even necessary practice, self-observation.

Present to the Dream

We often reject the present moment because what is arising in the present moment doesn't seem very "present" to us [*i.e.,* daydreaming]. Most of us aren't "present" all the time in the context with which we could define "Presence." What about all the time when we are not in that "Presence" state? Does it mean we are not present? No. The practice is to be with what is, as it is, here and now. That phrase does not say, "Accept what is, as it is, only when you feel that it is 'Presence' within the most enlightened definition of the word 'Presence.'" It doesn't say, "Accept what is, except the exceptions." There are no exceptions! Accept what *is* as it is, includes *anything*. If it is purely relative in the moment, then that's what it is, as it is— relative! If it's imagination, projection, daydreaming, that's what it is. Accept what is, as it is, here and now. When you catch yourself daydreaming, or whatever, instead of saying, "I'm not present, I want to be present," simply be present as you are, which in that case is daydreaming.

Know Your Character

The teacher EJ Gold says that there are many "characters" in us, including the "disciple." And we can choose which character we're going to animate. So, if a character is being animated that is not the character that we would like to be animated (like the "saboteur"), it is possible to choose another character. Because, if somebody said to any of us, what are the qualities of a disciple, for example, there would be various differences in our answer, but most of us would have a pretty clear idea of how we would define "disciple." In a technical sense, it is just as easy to animate the disciple character as it is to animate the "saboteur" or the "rageoholic."

The more intimately you know any other character, the easier it will be not to allow that character to interfere. So, it's back to ruthless self observation.

Seek Resolution

My idea is not to clarify people's confusion or to give people answers that are satisfying. My idea is to create an irritation, a disturbance. If it means enough to you to come to resolve, then you've got all the necessary tools and gifts and the necessary consciousness to come to resolve. If the resolution of this kind of irritation does not mean that much to you, you'll [read some other book], go to some other teacher or some other seminar in which you'll be consoled, and then your mind will be satisfied and you'll just pretend that there never was an irritation.

Lay Down Your Sword

———

For most of us, it takes twenty years just to get to a place of real vulnerability. Most of us have to get personally shattered, but it doesn't *have* to work that way. You can come to a state of tenderness and vulnerability without that kind of a fight, but you've got to pay the price. You've got to lay down your sword. You've got to take off your armor. If you don't lay down the sword and take off the armor, the only way you're going to get it is in the jousting ring.

Fear's Defense

———

You can get as drunk or "high" as you want, but you always come back and remember. Every time you attempt to obliterate the thing that causes the fear, or when you declare war on it, or try to beat it up, it just gears up for defense. The fear becomes more apparent to you when you do "come down," and soon it becomes so obvious that it's consuming you that you must work even harder to try to forget it again.

Feel Their Pain

As adults, we need to be able to feel into a child's or teenager's viewpoint in order to understand how best to define limits. For example, when a thirteen-year-old breaks up with her first boyfriend, to us it may not be a problem. We may even be quite relieved. We've had love affairs, and to us it's like, "You'll get over it. You're young. You'll have plenty more chances." We have perspective, but they don't. To them, breaking up is a very big deal. To them, their entire social life for the next six years depends upon this situation. If we can't feel into their position, we will fail them in being sympathetic and in dealing with their emotions satisfactorily. If a child needs something, we may not drop everything we are doing and run to them, but if we can't feel into their viewpoint we would be unlikely to handle their needs in a way that worked for both ourselves and them, and they are likely to become increasingly frustrated.

Surround Yourself With Beauty

Okay, you aren't enlightened. You aren't transformed. You aren't saving the world. The world is still full of violence and aggression; the air and the water and the earth are all polluted. You can't take care of the world, so just take care of *your* world. In your personal space, surround yourself with beauty of any kind. Do anything you can to surround yourself with beauty, harmonious relationships, sacred space and beautiful art, because that's what we have.

No Luxury

———

Practice is not a luxury; it is a very real necessity. Not only do *our* lives depend on it, but perhaps even the lives of all sentient creatures, at least to some degree. You certainly wouldn't shrug your shoulders with an "Oh well, that's life" if your children were in real danger. You'd jump to the need and put yourself on the line.

You Must Act

———

There is only one way to change a pattern of negative thinking. You must act. What is action? An apology, a look, a touch, a word. Logical thought will never change an emotion. Action will. Don't sit and stew when you are jealous or angry. Work, sing, go and say something nice to someone. When some people feel sorry for themselves they sit down and stare at the walls. Instead, go do something else!

Enlightenment

How do we get enlightened? You listen to those who are telling the truth, even though the world may be saying that they are liars, because the world is threatened by the truth. Then, as the Christians say, charity begins at home. You start at the lowest level of practice, and when that level is absolutely reliable, you move to the next level of practice. The Dalai Lama gets up at three o'clock every morning and practices until seven o'clock every morning—*every* morning. That is *reliable* practice, and without reliable practice, you will not build the structure on which enlightenment must stand. Although there is no such thing as enlightenment; there is what I call "Enlightened Duality." Enlightened Duality is Reality, and without a practice that is reliable, we will never realize it.

God Serves in Relationship

The Divine, or God, responds not as a great and kindly father helping his children, but in the *form* of human possibility or ultimate human capacity. God doesn't "help" humanity with thunderbolts and lightning, with magic, but with the human expression of Divine qualities towards other human beings. God serves in *relationship,* in the interaction between individuals and individuals and things, not in some mythical and supernatural way.

Feel the Love

———

"Feel the love" that is the essence of the Path, the Core of existence itself, the defining element of Creation. "Feel the love" that is God's Self-reflection, the purpose of being, the Radiance that is Truth, that is Creation. "Feel the love." Don't wait for me, or anyone else for that matter, to demonstrate it. *You:* "feel the love." It is always available, always accessible, it is, in fact, not other than yourself, so *you*, yes *you*: "feel the love." Never mind that the new age, not to mention the advertising world, has co-opted this little walnut, and turned it into a meaningless psycho-babble of a cliché. Never mind. Do you, yes *you*, want what Life in its Objective fullness can offer or what? If your answer is "yes," "Feel the love." Don't wait on your guru, don't wait on your lover, don't wait on God! "Feel the love."

Sublime Longing

In the ordinary world of emotional love, missing someone—
which we could call longing in its small sense—is usually seen
as a problem, an annoyance, more than likely because, unlike
our orders at Burger King, we cannot "have it our way." We
think that if we can't control the situation that things must turn
out badly, must be a struggle. But in the mystical world, in the
realm of the worship of the Divine, the Personal God, longing,
even for a human lover, can be so sublime, so startlingly
infused with even the literal physical sensations of fulfillment
and pleasure, as to be, in many cases, even more acute than
actual physical contact. This in no way indicates that physical
contact is altogether transcended or denied (which when it
is, is just another form of intimacy-denying pathology), for
physical intimacy has its own sweet and fulfilling dimensions
to it. Longing isn't necessarily a sign that anything is lacking or
not right. When life gives us longing, we can give longing life
and turn it into another facet of our deepening and expanding
love. Not only will our minds, our hearts and our very cells
approve, so will God!

Watering the Seed
(for Yogi Ramsuratkumar)

———

Yogi Ramsuratkumar
     You dirty Madman—
this seed You planted in my heart
     is watered by the tears I shed over You,
     and warmed by the sun of Your touch,
and grows to be with You.
     Your son sings Your praise
through the flute of his broken heart.

Energy Management

The amount of energy needed to negatively obsess or neurotically indulge or dramatize or to keep you well buffered and resistant to not only the Teaching but to peace of mind and equanimity of body and emotion as well, is the exact amount of energy needed to surrender to the Will of God. So, in every moment of recoil and rejection of the Divine, you could be communing with and embracing (being embraced by) the Divine. This energy cannot do both at the same time, so as long as it is allocated for the animation of the cramp and posture of survival, as defined by the initial primal psychological knot, it is inaccessible to That which would and can allocate it for Submission or Service to God. The energy itself is neutral, it has no essential bias or disposition, but is simply used according to the Gesture of its "director." It takes, in another way of saying it, no more energy to Awaken or to Realize than it does to stay asleep or willfully maintain the illusion of separation, thereby generating ceaseless suffering and self-centeredness.

Knowing Our Tendencies

—

We associate trusting ourselves with pure qualities like generosity and love for all beings, and if we don't feel those we don't trust ourselves. But trusting ourselves is about knowing who we are, not who we think we should be or are supposed to be. In my own case I'm tremendously impressed with famous people. I'm reliable in that way—I know who I am in that, and that I will respond in that way, but I also know how to draw boundaries around that response. Trusting ourselves is knowing who we are, not just to look for these pure, perfect expressions of humanity in ourselves.

Who Is Awake?

What really defines the awakened state is an awakened condition that is stable over long periods of time, like a lifetime, and present at all times. The rare spikes out of ego into ego-transcendence—as long as those spikes fall back into ego again—is nothing but an isolated experience, one of the infinite number of experiences every human being is always having. Awakening is an objective state, true at all levels of consciousness and being, not simply the theoretical or subtle levels of higher mind. We must learn to make distinctions and to observe ourselves with ruthless self-honesty, to have patience and not to impulsively leap to absurd conclusions because of a little spurt of bliss or insight. We must deeply study the protocols of the Path so as not to be caught, blindsided by the temptation of ego to power, spiritual authority and wisdom based on empty or even rotten foundations. In short, we need to grow up and be sane.

The Work Takes Care of Us

—

When we take care of the Work, the Work takes care of us. How do we take care of the Work? In principle: selfless sacrifice—develop compassion relative to all creation. And charity starts at home.

Becoming One With

When we get opened up a little bit we don't get to pick and choose what we become sensitive to. We become sensitive to beauty and art, but darkness, pain and suffering also become more intense for us. It's a heavy burden to bear, this darkness and misery that invades us when we open up. Even if we're not conscious of it, when we open up, we open up to everything. If you are sensitive you're going to have to figure out how to deal with all the cruelty, injustice and pain in the world. If you keep your natural sense of wonder and awe and beauty alive, you'll also cross paths with much joy and profound happiness, but you'll have to learn how to deal with both. You approach them both the same way, which we don't want to have to do, which is to "become one with" in the words of Swami Prajnanpad, because to "become one with" gives everything the same flavor: *ananda*.

The Interconnected Cosmos of Beings

The piercing of the knot that holds the dilemma of survival and seeking firmly in place is a matter of seeing who one is. However, the "one" that is seen is not some exclusive individual, but a whole, moving, feeling, interconnected cosmos of beings and things, and more beings and more things, and all of the texture and laws that unite all the seemingly illogical pieces in a big, even more illogical, jigsaw puzzle. We are not other than the whole of creation. We are simply just not "other."

More Than Perfection?

———

Usually, when things are perfect, and we try to make them *more* perfect, all we get is imperfect, which makes us feel disturbed, dissonant and confused. So, what if when we hit that perfect moment we just ceased altogether our grasping attempts to go forward?

256

Give It Away

———

The only way something really becomes "ours" is when we give it up in the appropriate way. "It is more blessed to give than receive" because it is impossible to receive in a true way without giving that thing first.

257

Just This, Again!

———

Just This. One of the struggles of the path is that we keep trying to relate to reality based on the habit of relating to past and future. There is no such thing as the past, and there is no such thing as the future, except in our minds. The past did exist, but it doesn't now, and the future does not exist, therefore it's academic.

Decisions Matter

———

We are making decisions all the time—about what we eat, what we read, what movies we see. It is our responsibility to pay attention to the basis on which we make decisions as if there were no separation between our practice and our dharma and anything that has to do with our lives: public school, children, profession, travel, wherever we find ourselves, even shopping in WalMart. There shouldn't be any separation, but we haven't completely come to terms with our unconscious yet.

We need to affirm to ourselves, "Everything that my life is about, from the most mundane to sitting for meditation in the morning, is not separate from the holistic process of having found my Path or my guru, and having begun to practice in very particular ways." The decisions we make should be based on dharma, not on the materialistic momentum that culture and society has been inundating us with for years.

Love One Another, Love God

Surrender to the Will of God is the foundation of a True spiritual culture. In the midst of the purification naturally encouraged by the demand to surrender to the Will of God, and by the ongoing process of sympathy to that, one must *consider* Loving God through bodily, emotional and mental relationship to one another, with care and love and compassion and consideration.

The physical situations of our lives may vary immensely, may become more comfortable or more trying, but none of that is more than incidental. Your focus must cease to be the context of your search for release and desire-fulfillment, and must become the *active consideration* of Loving God.

Sex Is Non-Problematical

———

Essentially, sexuality is nonproblematical. It only becomes problematical when it becomes a means to an end rather than "just what it is" freely. The lineage that I'm associated with— the Bauls of Bengal—believes that the way to realization of God is *through* the body, not through denial or renunciation. This is called *Kaya Sadhana*. That means, that as long as we have a body it's a shame to waste good equipment...or let it rust or atrophy.

Don't deny your sexuality, therefore, and don't exaggerate, dramatize, or indulge it either. Allow your sexuality to respond naturally and spontaneously without artifice in relationship to the space, the mood, the circumstance, and the environment. Sexuality is not a law unto itself. It doesn't make its own rules irrespective of every other factor in the environment (although our minds act as if it should).

Live in the Present Moment

───

We can´t exactly define enlightenment—we can only imply or talk around it. One definition is to live in the present moment. One way to do that is to accept what is, here and now. That doesn't mean that we don't have personal volition, it means that how things are now in this moment can't be any different than they are. That is the physics of things. But in the next moment things can be different. To accept what is does not say anything about the future. If, in this moment, we are not accepting what is, we are either living in the past and our future will not be a function of Reality but of the past, or we are dysfunctional in the moment. To accept what is, as it is, here and now could be a kind of formula for living an enlightened life—a framework against which to measure ourselves. How awake are we? We´re either living in the present moment or not, in which case we are asleep. We´re either clear or under illusion. We can´t be partly under illusion.

A Sacred Act

Sex is a sacred act, and should be treated as a sacred act every time, which doesn't mean you should only have sex twice a year either. The frequency is irrelevant. Whether sex is engaged every day, once a month, twice a month, or once a year, it is a sacred act. A conscious man or a conscious woman, someone with some real sensitivity, who is basically mature at the level of the third chakra (the sexual center) or above (at the level of the heart, etc.), holds within himself or herself the power for sex to be an entry or a doorway. That possibility should never be trampled upon. Union between a conscious man and a conscious woman is always sacred. And, admittedly, any consideration of sexuality, just like any consideration of spiritual life, will need to recognize the dilemmas and the problems that we face in this area.

Survival

Survival (or actually the constant threat to survival) is the ground from which humans move, from which they relate to all events in their lives. It's not that people walk out on the street, look up and down and say, "Cars could kill me." People think *from* that condition. When someone gets up in the morning, as soon as they are conscious, they are thinking *from* survival. Everything is a threat. Everything is seen as a threat automatically, with no critical perspective at all. This ground or context is how everything and everyone is approached, as if the very next thing, experience or person could be the instrument of termination for the being.

Children and the Divine

I have noticed that every child has an instinctual relationship to the divine, some very natural, relaxed and ordinary, some profoundly mystical and visionary. But in any case, this relationship merely needs to be accepted, acknowledged, and appropriately set in context (by adults, or the enlightened witness, à la Alice Miller). It does not need to be re-defined or trained into a specific form of religious ritual or routine. I could wish nothing greater for the children of the devotees of this community than for them to be happy, full of radiance and brightness throughout their lives, having integrity and impeccability in their dealings and relationships, and being grounded and certain in their own individual relationship to the Divine whether that relationship manifests within the context of a practicing spiritual Tradition, this or any other one, or whether it manifests in their own personal expression to and with and towards all creatures and all things. The legacy I would like to leave my children and all children is one of love and gratitude.

More Temptation

We earn spiritual authority based on the strength of our practice, and the more spiritual authority we have, the more temptation there will be. The more power you have, the more opportunities you will have to sell out, so you'd better know yourself. Whoever we are, we never know when a temptation will be thrown in our path. At a high level, we cannot play around—there are serious consequences for selling out. So, each of us has a responsibility to ourselves, to the Path, to the teacher and to God, really, not to sell out. We have to know what our weaknesses are.

Everything Could Be Different

One of the things that makes us uncomfortable is that we think we should be different. "Oh, I shouldn't make mistakes, be so forgetful, whatever." But what is, is. And if we can accept that, through self-observation and ruthless self-honesty, then the next moment is not conditioned or predictable, and includes the possibility that anything or even everything could be different.

Timing

—

Usually we think right timing must be associated with a feeling of completion. Actually it is the opposite. Right timing is always a function of what serves God in the moment, and feelings of completion are what serve ego in the moment. If one IS functioning in a context of Reality (we could say in an awakened condition or state, but it isn't that simple) then "feeling complete" is a non-existent phenomenon. There isn't any such thing. And if we are functioning in a context of ego (are any of you not?) then right-timing usually feels incomplete. Well, I hope that has been helpful because as every comedian knows: "Timing is everything."

Beauty Builds Something Real

Someone once said that it is better to have loved and lost than never to have loved at all; that's true because every time we love, it builds something in us that creates truth, reality and an abiding relationship to the Universe. If you have ever really loved, something has been built in you that cannot be taken away, even when the body dies. Every time you have a conscious experience of objective beauty, something in you grows and progresses.

Instructions for Kundalini Experience

Just because you're in an altered state of consciousness doesn't mean that you are on the Path. With kundalini yoga, for example, it's possible to be thrust into a state of consciousness where you could be unable to function in normal ways, not be able to take care of yourself, but those kinds of experiences are not signs of success on the Path. They are not even that unusual. They usually happen to people who approach the Path without any guidance or foundation whatsoever. Some of my students have entered into extreme, deep and ecstatic experiences in which they could have meditated for days, weeks, months. There is a physical pull to abandon everything and go into the experience, but typically this is not what's called for. My instruction has been to not withdraw from work or family, but to internalize the experience. At the same time, don't compromise or suppress the experience, but interiorize it as much as possible.

Draw No Conclusions Mind

———

There are two ways to come to some resolve about this problem of mind. First, you find the primal moment in which you developed a survival strategy, bringing your adult intelligence and rational objectivity to that point and using it to choose a positive, and even ecstatic strategy, instead.

The second possibility is to simply sever the mind's relationship to conclusive or analytical thinking. The mind is like a computer that analyzes every bit of stimuli picked up by the senses. It then selects the stimuli that reinforce survival, and rejects what doesn't. If you sever the mind's analytical process, you have a senile and impotent dictator, just a figurehead with no power whatsoever. That alternative is the one that I would support. It's also the easier of the two.

This severing process is, in my language, "Draw No Conclusions Mind." Psychological work has its value, but it's literally endless. Draw No Conclusions Mind is still the best bet!

The Delicate Moment

Sooner or later the mind will seek a deeper process. All by itself. Instead of gross physical distractions, it will then attempt to use more powerful and seductive means to fascinate us, distract us, or control us. If, however, we do not give it what it demands—if we do not indulge the fascination, the distraction, the demands to be controlled, but rather use the distractions as reminding factors, after a while the mind will go to the most powerful of its sources, to the point of inception, the literal source of its own arising.

When you reach that point, you are on the borderline between two very distinct dynamics. On one side you find the dynamic of ego, the whole autonomous, mechanical *definition* that mind itself creates and sustains, and on the other side is the energy that we call the Will of God.

Then there is a possibility of either going back on the side of ego, or falling onto the side of the Will of God. It's a very delicate moment.

Dignity Is Its Own Reward

What a sweet and soul-satisfying presence is a person with dignity. How much sweeter when you are such a person. Please do not continue to suffer the constant indignity of the "blah, blah, blah." As Swami Prajnanpad said, we are all intrinsically noble and intrinsically dignified, so this is not something we must develop. It is something we must discover and allow through its dynamic attractiveness to override mechanical habits—self-love of the sound of our own voice, the feeling we know better, the urge to intrude, dominate, and aggress upon the other, insecurities that drive us to desperately "blah, blah, blah." Dignity is its own reward. Dignity is its own payoff.

Action, Action!

In Orthodox Judaism, hospitality is a high law, and acts are prized over internal considering. Abraham (of Bible note) was sitting in front of his house in ecstatic communion with God when he happened to notice several travelers passing by on the road. He jumped up immediately and ran to them to offer them a drink, a meal, some rest. Abraham broke off his inner conversation with God Himself in order to act.

Live Full Out

———

Life needs no help, no artificial creations, no push or pull, none of our idea of what would be a strong enough shock to start, or restart, or even continue a process of dissolution, of the disintegration of the fortress of denial, blindness, unconsciousness. Life itself will provoke the crisis that effects the realization, the deep and certain knowledge of our hopelessness. So? Just live. Live full out, not following your dreams of creative success, financial success, sexual prowess or the search for love, thrills, chills and pills, *no*! Live full out according to what life gives freely of its own largess and wisdom, un-niggled by our urging, demands, ostensible prayers, whining and needling. Just live full out through meeting life openly, with a willingness to be moved, up, down or sideways, to be pierced to the core.

Life will do the preparatory work. Life will make the initial gestures and needs you to pick up from where the groundwork leaves off and take it to the next, and all the next levels right up to the level that only Grace can define and Realize. So relax, be patient, and be ready to leap when life says jump.

Stay with the Irritation

The mind/body unit naturally moves toward harmony. If there is any kind of disturbance of the mind/body, the way to move through it is to *stay with it*. The usual tendency is to suppress or avoid anything that threatens us. If you stay with the irritant, the body will provide the natural means to move through it because the body seeks harmony. Whatever thread you are able to keep alive, keep your attention there and the body will move the irritation through.

Happy Together

———

Something is terribly wrong. We shouldn't even be talking about the Work if we aren't happy in one another's company. It doesn't matter if someone breaks a plate or a glass with our monogram on it. Whatever we hold precious, it doesn't matter. If we cannot be happy in one another's company, regardless of what goes on, the Work doesn't mean a thing.

A Teaching Story from Sanatan Das Baul Thakur

———

A young man was struggling with his guru, who suggested he go to learn from King Janaka, universally renowned as a wise sage, a saint and an extraordinary Teacher. The young man, very orthodox and serious, was thrilled. When ushered into Janaka's presence, he sees him surrounded by beautiful naked women, opulent clothing and lush trappings, waited on hand and foot; he is completely shocked. But, remembering Janaka's sterling reputation, and having committed to studying with him, he stays. After a few weeks, with the young renunciate still at a loss for what is going on, a vast fire erupts and threatens to burn down the entire palace. King Janaka doesn't seem to notice and continues to teach as if nothing is going on. However, the young man remembers that his spare loincloth is in his room, begins to panic and bolts from the Teaching Chamber. After the fire has been contained and they are back together, the King says to the student, "Here we are, and I, whose entire kingdom was being lost remained calm and detached while you, who had nothing to lose but a loincloth, were completely attached." And that was the lesson.

Be Bored

We have to come to terms with what happens if we just sit with our boredom. The next time you're bored, literally just stay there. Don't try to do anything about it. Don't dramatize or indulge it. Just stay there, as long as it takes—ten minutes, ten days—until it changes into something else. Before it changes into something else, you may have some scary thoughts go through your mind. Don't let those thoughts stop you from being really bored. When it changes, you will be amazed—not horrified—at what it changes into.

You want the boredom to be pervasive, complete, total, so that when it changes into something else it will be complete, total, pervasive. If you let your mind distract you from boredom, you'll never get to what you can get to. So, we have to practice, practice, practice, time after time, to not allow the mind to take us away from the intention we have for transformation.

But, you have to persist. Like an athlete, if you keep running and don't stop, sooner or later . . . the zone! You're not tired, your breath comes naturally, like a panther, and you can run for days! Aahhh!

A Simple Solution
(for Yogi Ramsuratkumar)

Oh Father Yogi Ramsuratkumar,
    everyone wants bliss
but who wants to pay the price?
    And what is the price?
Simply to refuse to blame others
    as if they were the cause
of our own suffering.
    No more, no hidden costs,
simply this small concession:
    To be ruthlessly honest
about our failure
    to let go on our misery.
Just This, Just This, Just This.

Accumulate Merit

———

Life surely and certainly is not limited to our infinitesimally short blink-of-an-eye time here in this body, as this finite character on this planet. Life was before, and life goes on in a great and fluid continuum. Yes? And so it would seem to me to make sense to "lay up stores for the future" so to speak—call it the accumulation of merit or the generation of good Karma, if you will or wish—and to pay close care to even the smallest or slightest detail in our daily existence, for nothing is too minor to overlook or neglect when it comes to the effect of that sloppiness in the Holy World of God.

Too Much Caution

———

How we love to complicate matters, adding superimposition upon superimposition on the bare simple situation. Too much caution based upon muscular (mental, emotional or physical) effort actually handicaps whatever process we are engaged in. Caution based on fear, on shoulds, on our neurotic need to be "good," to do the right thing, albeit honest and sincere in principle, in practice tends towards counter-productivity. We want to take down walls and yet we actually put more up, strengthening the ones already in place. We desire openness and vulnerability and yet actually close off and shut down.

Every Cell Will Sing
(for Yogi Ramsuratkumar)

The only important thing
   is that every cell in this body
sings "Yogi Ramsuratkumar" without cease
   to the ends of time and space.

Have Intention

———

Shams-E-Tabriz's pithy statement—"On this way, to die with the longing to attain one's longing is also a great work"—refers to the obvious practice of intention, and taking each day as it comes, without relying on some imagined goal or fixed result. To die longing, when that longing is based on Faith, devotion, gratitude, and wisdom, may well be to have attained one's longing. It is the essence of one's being that gets "counted" in Heaven, not necessarily the spiritual goodies that one has collected.

Keep Your Sense of Humor

A sense of humor keeps you from getting caught up in all the drama. When you are not identifying with the drama in your life, you can enjoy the play, whether it is a comedy, tragedy, or musical. When you identify with the drama it becomes very real for you, and it reinforces separation.

Spontaneity

If you practice self-observation and vigilance correctly, you will not have to do anything else: everything that will be revealed to you out of your vigilance will make your body act in a way that will be very natural and spontaneous. Spontaneity does not come from trying to be spontaneous at all costs, it comes from observing yourself as you are, not as you are in your divine essence, but now, totally, and on all levels. If you can see yourself in that way, the innate wisdom, life itself, starts to water your garden and spontaneity shoots up like a well-cared-for flower.

No Problem Mind

There's no problem, why make a problem? At least there is no problem *now*. If you insist on creating a problem I'm afraid there is nothing I can do about it. But you don't have to! Try it. Try *not vivifying a problem*. It might seem a little strange at first, since if we have a habit of creating problems, as soon as we stop creating them we feel ill at ease; like something is wrong. But, it is obvious that if we have two options—problem and no problem—the better of two options is no problem. If we stay with this option, after a while it feels comfortable and it fits. It's a viable option, why not?

No Sweet Goodbye

The great masters never consoled their disciples. Jesus knew that he was going to die, and he asked his disciples to stay with him in the Garden of Gethsemane for his last night with them. He told them to stay awake while he went to pray, but when he came back they were asleep. And instead of leaving them with a nice memory and saying, "It's okay, you're only human. It happens once in a while, " he said, "You feel asleep? Couldn't my closest disciples stay up for one hour?" He always criticized them. He said to Peter, "You will deny me." Peter said, "No, no, I won't!" Jesus said, "Yes you will. When your life is on the line, you are not going to think of me." So, even right at the end, when he knew that he would be leaving his disciples, he didn't give them any comfort. He didn't give them the last memory of a pat on the shoulder and a sympathetic goodbye.

Judgments Lock Us In

We need to see ourselves as we are *without judgment*—not to pat ourselves on the back (for something positive), or only to see negative things. All those judgments are just personality. To make a judgment about one frame in the movie doesn't in any way reflect the whole movie. Simply see things as they are, because in the next instant it can be different; in one moment we were selfish, and in the next we were compassionate! Any judgment locks us into what is categorically untrue.

Money Management

———

Some people are "penny wise, pound foolish," others may be "penny foolish, pound wise." Now if you are "penny wise, pound wise" you're probably just a trifle tight so *loosen up*. Wisdom does not include tight-fistedness, fear of loss or of spending, survival-panic, manipulation of others or using the resources of others for your own benefit.

If you are "penny foolish, pound foolish" you probably need *serious therapy* and don't bother taking a money management seminar, it is your mind that needs the management. If you are "penny wise, pound foolish," don't be impulsive in large financial decisions, do your research, don't live above your means, simply reverse your focus to "penny foolish, pound wise." Then, there's no need to do anything because all the pennies you save by being pound-wise will far exceed the pennies you spend foolishly. So, "don't sweat the small stuff" because as many of you know, to sweat the small stuff makes you belligerent and unhappy and causes great stress and tension, not only to you but to all involved.

Bring on the Tidal Wave

When some fact about oneself is seen only in the head, with the intellect or perceptive faculties alone, it may be seen with the most accurate (even frightening) clarity and detail, but it hasn't truly been seen if one is not "being different" about that activity, naturally and easefully, from then on. An intellectual sighting is no more than a ripple in the water, where a tidal wave is needed. One cannot be compassionate or in synchronization with the Law with mere "head" knowledge.

The Presumption of Separation

There's only ever one problem—the presumption of separation. Everything else is an extrapolation of the one problem. Everybody knows that, and everybody has the same problem. Everything else we think to be problems are facets of that. We assume if something in life is not to our liking, something must be wrong. In life there are ups, downs, highs, lows, good and bad. If life was the way *we* wanted it to be, it would be so bland it would be unbearable. Anger, fear, discomfort are not problems. The problem is that we are unable to accept anger, fear, discomfort. We're always assuming division when the fact of life is unity. It's purely a problem of our perception. And it's not really a problem because it is illusion. It's empty. Separation is not the problem, the *presumption of separation* is the problem because the presumption can be changed. So there is no problem. It's all made up in our minds.

Give In

"Give in so as to conquer" is the principle in judo, and also the principle in "winning." If you really want to win, if you really want to master a situation, you have to give in and allow that situation itself to transcend its own limitations and resistances. It will, if you apply this principle properly.

Overpowering everything is not the way. The way to win or master a situation is through ruthless softness and uncompromising gentleness. The women who did that best in the annals of history are the women who had real power. Women who could humble the greatest poets, the greatest writers, and the greatest warriors were women who knew how to "give in so as to conquer."

The Problem Serves You

Your very suffering keeps showing you that you are suffering. It is your catalyst. If you were perfectly satisfied and had no problems, would you be doing any real spiritual work? The very thing that was the content of the problem, which is the search, becomes the burr under the saddle that serves your awakening. It continues to serve your sadhana by constantly pointing you to what is *not* the case in relationship to context.

Wisdom

———▼———

Wisdom is a ground, a context, of how we view life and reality; spiritual practices are specifics that help us to move with and in life and reality with ease, confidence, and tacit realization of what is true and accurate, over and against what is false and subjective—in other words, our ego stories.

Real Life

Real Life is about having the tension-to-survive undermined moment to moment by the freedom to simply exist.

Offer Yourself

Besides the external, the other level of giving to the Work is internal. I mean a willingness to offer everything that you are to be used by the Work, whatever that is, whatever that means, whatever the consequences. The offer comes without strings attached—it's not a business deal. So you offer yourself to the Work for whatever the Work wants you for, without regard for the consequences.

In other words, everything we have is a gift. When we offer ourselves to the Work without regard for consequences (and that's the only way the Work will accept our offer), then there is no guarantee as to whether we get to be financially successful and have love, beauty, family in our lives—all the things the average person wants. You have to offer yourself up, no strings attached. The Work doesn't always take your offer. Sometimes psychotics come to the Work and offer themselves up, but the Work doesn't want them because it's not profitable in the long run.

Jesus and Forgiveness

When Jesus spoke, "Forgive them Father, for they know not what they do," he was asking that ego, mind, that blind unconsciousness, that forgetting who human beings are, and who God is, be forgiven. To the seeming end, Jesus was most deeply compassionate and surrendered to the need for humankind to become aware, awake, and intentioned. He wasn't as concerned that the crowd was killing him as that his death wouldn't serve their understanding of the law or their love of God. So he asked his dear Father to forgive them anyway, not for their actions but for their delusion of self-meditation and self-absorption. Such is the way of a True Man of God.

In the Details

It's much easier to be a hero than it is to submit little things to the fire of spiritual work.

Progress in Small Things

It is common that in our imagination we see ourselves, relative to practice, doing big things, making great gestures, even fulfilling tasks heroically (to much praise and applause) or, for those of us full of self-hatred and insecurity, just the opposite: we see ourselves, relative to practice, failing miserably and doing, accomplishing nothing (to much criticism and to the disappointment of others). In either case, what we are missing is the simple moment-to-moment clarity generated by the awareness of who we are, what we are doing, and *why*. It is the small things, which can make the big differences in the breakthroughs in practice and consciousness, in fact, that can fuel our confidence and momentum on the Path. The profound insights, the explosive breakthroughs, the momentous revelations, they will come in the course of our efforts, but those things should not dissuade us from the natural, every-day, day in and day out, need to pay attention and continue to develop a deeper and more cutting self-knowledge.

The Greatest Teacher

Someone asked the Dalai Lama who his greatest teacher was and he said Mao Tse Tung, because the Dalai Lama was forced to develop compassion under circumstances that were unique. He said that if it hadn't been for those circumstances, he might not have been such a compassionate man. That is very impressive. When Nelson Mandela was released from prison, he was asked if he had hatred and anger toward the jailors who had beaten him in a dehumanizing situation. He said, "If I allow myself to be angry with them, then they win," meaning that violence and abuse of authority would win over compassion and intelligence. If we are transparent to the Divine—so that we are able to manifest qualities such as kindness, gentleness, compassion, humility and understanding in spite of circumstances that are psychologically provocative—we could say that we are *outshined* by the Divine. It is our job on the Path to be outshined by God, so that God becomes so bright that we become invisible.

Do the Right Thing

Honor is such a truly glorious quality, such a moving demonstration of the real essence of "intrinsic nobility and intrinsic dignity" as Swami Prajnanpad called it, of Chögyam Trungpa's "basic goodness." The lack of honor as a quality in a person's behavior—the demonstrations of the lies, the madness, the desperation, the pettiness, the grotesque twists and turns impaled upon the sword point of survival-fears or power-greed in its various guises—is so ugly, such a corruption of the human spirit, so detestable, abhorrent, pitiable and foolish that how could one not, in principle, choose to "do the right thing," if of course one were conscious enough and present enough to recognize the choices, the options? Ah yes, *in principle*. Would *I* "do the right thing" under stressful enough conditions? Maybe not.

In any event, taste it (honor) so you may know that it is Divine Nectar, manna. Maybe this is even one of the qualities that makes us human, that distinguishes us from simply being just another species of mammal. In any event, I wish you all most honorable lives.

The Doorway to the Divine

———

In Baul sexual practice, partner practice, in which Radha and Krishna are the ultimate symbols of union with God, when the man is with his wife or thinking of her, he thinks of her as Radha, and she thinks of him as Krishna. So, whenever they are together, sexually, or just sitting before the fire talking about the grandkids, there is an objective mood of adoration.

The instruction is to relate to the human being as if Radha or Krishna is the *doorway* to union with the Divine, but they are not the same thing.

Only Relationship

People commonly think they want a relationship, but there is no such thing as "a relationship." There is only *relationship*. There is no *relationship* when you have "a relationship." This is an esoteric, dharmic consideration of language. But it is also true. It's also a contradiction in terms: "*A* relationship" denies what *relationship* is.

No Separate Self

———

Inner dissatisfaction can never be adequately dealt with through entertainment or distraction no matter how demanding, addictive, flashy, those distractions are. If one wishes to actually be free of the dread of that nebulous, shadowy, ever-present, hovering something-or-other, and free of the dread of running out of distraction material and finding oneself face to face with, *with what?*, one must pierce the illusion that there is someone—some substantial, permanent, separate "one"—that is feeling whatever it is that has created this inner turmoil, be it self-hatred, fear, unlove, insecurity, or any other desperate need for attention and acknowledgement. To pierce this illusion requires a commitment, a self-honesty that seems a bit beyond the average person's willingness to engage. There is a willingness of intention, but rarely is it backed up by the willingness to "pay the piper," to do what is necessary to actually effect the elements of being that would allow this piercing of illusion to come to mature fruition. So, we cannot sugarcoat the mood of either lacking something essential, or of needing to seek to find the missing element— one mood passive, the other aggressive—both, in the end, or in the beginning, the same thing. What to do?

Perfect Pristine Awareness

You are a holistic being: mind, emotions, feelings, aura, causal mind, astral mind, etheric mind—all of that is a part of you, holistically, but none of it *is* you. You are non-problematical, tacit awareness of Reality, completely transcendent to time and space. Transcending time and space means in every moment, without effort, in a natural process. Awareness *is*. We don't have to do anything about awareness. Awareness has been covered up with layer after layer after layer. The typical metaphor is the onion—you peel one layer, then there is another and another and another.

When you interrupt the pattern, it creates a crack in all the layers, and at the base of that crack is you as perfect, pristine awareness. Whenever there is even an instantaneous crack in the pattern, you have the opportunity of being that which is already perfectly aware. None of the rest of the layers disappear necessarily, but they stop dominating and running you. That's the point.

Play the Game

When we play Bridge, we are playing a card game. It behooves us to pay attention to *the cards*, since it's a card game. Whether we play well or poorly is certainly an element of our personal presence at the table, but none of our psychological dross has anything to do with the *cards*. I suppose we could use this as a metaphor for the Work, the Path, for Sadhana. It would behoove us to pay attention to *that* (or That), to the game we've chosen, instead of to our self-hatred, insecurities, etc.

Heartbreak on Heartbreak

If one is going to let this Work devour you—the only reasonable solution to the age-old dilemma of the illusion of separation, the delusion of independent existence—such a one better get used to heartbreak, because it is a state you will have to live with perhaps forever. As the implication of the Bodhisattva vow impacts you, you come to understand that suffering is endless and it is your sworn duty to devote your life to helping others "lighten the load," so to speak—a truly heartbreaking task for many reasons, not the least of which is that so few will actually allow their load to be lightened, even if you are willing to take it on; and so few are even mildly interested, in a real practical sense, of taking the steps to lighten their own load, even if they are miserable, unhappy and in constant pain, physical or psychological. Now that, when you are touched by others' suffering, is heartbreaking.

Not To React

———

Every emotion is a reaction. *We* give them substance. *We* give them reality, body power, authority, when in fact they are nothing. They are reactions. If you start to look at any emotion by asking, "What is it? Where does it come from?" ultimately you will find that it is just a reaction. And, you will find that it is just as possible *not* to react as it is to react. Before the point of being carried away it's just as easy not to react as it is to react. Maybe you're fighting with your partner furiously, and all of a sudden something in your peripheral attention captures your attention, and you turn around and you see the look on the face of your child. Instantly, you're able to stop the wave. Your response to your child is more important than staying with your reaction.

You will want to *see* the reaction . . . the first reaction. And the way you see it is to relax and observe. If you struggle against it, then you won't be seeing it clearly. If you try to stop it, kill it, suffocate it, repress it, you are actually reinforcing it. Work with the idea of not reacting to any reaction.

Ordinary Life, Awaiting the Beloved

Perhaps serving the Work is simply demonstrating kindness and compassion to others in ordinary life. Each one of us has our own destiny and role in the Work. But the purpose is to serve the Work, not to live in some kind of exclusive mystical vacuum. When we realize this, life becomes very ordinary, maybe even boring. When the Beloved wants attention, or service, then the Beloved rings the bell and we walk through the door, but the opportunity doesn't present itself every day. We may go for long periods of time just living an ordinary life, practicing the principles of our work on the outside, while consumed with our Beloved within.

Trust Intrinsic Dignity

———

What's the worst thing that can happen if somebody is judging / criticizing / analyzing / nit-picking you and you don't react, go into recoil and assume that they hate you, think you're the slime of the earth, find your company distasteful, ugly, irritating and contemptible and snap their heads off? What if you just let it pass, making no projections and met whatever it was with love, spaciousness, amusement or acceptance without interpretation? Can you get a sense of how dramatically different the circumstance would be and how profoundly different the consequences of your response, both short-term and long-term, would be? Suspicion, the "looking for" that always expects the other person to be devious, harsh and aggressive, instead of innocent, even if at times a bit bitchy, is a costly emotion and/or mood. Why not trust the intrinsic dignity and intrinsic nobility of the other instead of investing so heavily in their psychology? Try it, you will be amazed and once you try it and *are* amazed, don't just throw it away, shrug it off, let it die the usual death of return to old habits, but keep that fresh and trusting faith alive and active.

Becoming Wiser

———

We might have an idea of life, if we really stop to think about what our projection is, of just maturing through great leaps and dramatic breakthroughs, but that's not it. Those things are fine if they move us into spaces where we can begin to appreciate one another more and handle our work in a better way. But that's not it. It's about a moment-to-moment genuine celebration in one another's company. That is a much more even kind of life, where our disposition remains essentially the same all the time: one of ease and gratitude and pleasure; where the changes of maturity that occur, must occur naturally and easefully in the context of our lives. We grow and we become wiser; we embrace more experience.

312

Divine Generosity

—◤—

Transformation on the spiritual path is about complete anni-
hilation in the Divine. Fortunately, the Divine is very gracious
and beneficent. If you give everything to the Divine—without
being guarded or without holding a little back just in case
you made a mistake—because what if you picked the "wrong
God?"—the Divine will make a return to you that is way
beyond what you have given.

Children First – The Higher Practice

If the predictable routines of our lives are interrupted by the moment-to-moment needs of our children, even if our special times are interrupted, I recommend that we spend the time helping and being with our children, and that we not put anything in front of the child's needs, unless we have to. That is the higher practice.

Heroic Practice

Eka understood that if a master as great as Bodhidharma was going to accept him as a disciple there would be some testing involved. So he just stood in front of Bodhidharma's hut. That night there was a snowstorm, right up to Eka's waist. But he just stood there without moving. And in the morning, Bodhidharma opens the door and sees him out there and says, "Well, that's not bad. But that's not going to make it." Slams the door. As the story goes, Eka pulls out his knife and cuts his left arm off at the elbow and throws his arm at Bodhidharma's door. This time, Bodhidharma opens the door, takes the arm, brings it inside, bakes it and has a wonderful dinner... *I'm kidding, I'm kidding!* Bodhidharma opens the door and says, "Clap your hands!"... *No!* ... He opens the door and he looks at Eka, and he says, "I guess you want it badly enough. Okay, come on in." And he teaches him. So, there is a time and a place for heroic practice.

Discover Yourself

———

When you die, or rather when your present physical form dissolves in what we call death, and you move elsewhere, you must realize that you cannot take the "other"—your belongings, your family, etc.—with you. The only one who always goes with you is *you*. I would recommend that you devote all of your life to discovering what "yourself" or who "yourself" is, so you will stop the foolish and fruitless relationships of fear, jealousy, and demanding, conflicting control that you have with your intimates and with the world at large and begin to live what few remaining years or months you have in love and devotion and ecstatic communion and surrender to God.

Just the Body

This thing we call the body, the vehicle for consciousness, for individuated consciousness with a self-reflective aspect to it, unlike plants, walls and chairs, is just weird. Just when you think you've got it where you want it, *blam*, a big pimple or *pow*, a whole mass of little dots or spots or uneven surfaces. It's always doing some little thing that isn't right, or is it? Well, folks, if you haven't gotten used to it by now, by now meaning that if you are old enough to read this you are old enough, yes; if you aren't used to it by now, *get used to it* because all those little abnormalities (or are they?) aren't going to stop, not anytime soon and maybe never. Lucky for us we don't live forever. Sooner or later, no matter how attached we are to this fleshy thing, it will go away and, hey, I wonder if there are all these kinds of blemish things on the other side, like on the subtle body?

Sparks and Flashes

If we think that flashes in the nervous system mean we have attained some realization, then we are probably fooling ourselves and will probably try to fool others. If, on the other hand, we understand that there is a vast encyclopedia of phenomena that are the sparks between the weak and temporal body and the flow of energy that is the Universe, then we might be able to make some use of our experience. The process of transformation is not just energetic or subtle, but an organic process in which the nervous system becomes capable of holding a greater charge of energy or spiritual force.

If we use the arising of phenomena to prove something to ourselves, we are handling it the wrong way. Transformation is not about momentary phenomena. It is about who we become after a lifetime of practice. The aim of the Path is to become a complete human being, involving relationships, the appreciation of beauty, and empathy for the suffering of others.

The Wound of Love

Humanity is suffering, and this condition has nothing to do with mistakes we've made. Maybe our mistakes have added a little bit of suffering in some domains, and maybe our successes have taken away a little bit in other domains, but life is suffering. That's what "heartbrokenness" has to do with, never with the past. Heartbrokenness has to do with what is now.

When you realize life is suffering, you also realize that there is only God—you realize the "Wound of Love"! So there is always the alternation between the "Wound of Love" and the "heartbrokenness" of suffering: You feel and are empathic with the suffering of humanity, and at the same time you realize that at some level we are all absolutely absorbed or subsumed by the Divine.

If Not You, Who?

For if we don't maintain sanity and equanimity and presence, not to mention Objective Work Conscience, who will? "We" as in this rare fraternity of those who are on the Path, in the Real World, in the Great Work. This is no time to turn your backs on sadhana and veg out, obsessed with supplements, videos, internet access and "personal space." I wouldn't go so far as to say that we are all called to be "caretakers" of the spiritual purity of the world or anything that grandiose, yet on the other hand there is a certain maintenance that has already fallen to us and those in like positions, and will to greater degrees as time goes by. Believe me, you will not want to get caught short (or napping).

True Friend
(for Yogi Ramsuratkumar)

———

lee, an arrogant Fool says this:
    seek only love
and Yogi Ramsuratkumar
    will be your Friend.

Seeking Is Suffering

The upgraded form of "the search" is the spiritual search. The average person searches for happiness by trying to fulfill his or her need systems in conventional ways: money, power, sex, possessions, and position. Transposing one's search from this "worldly" direction to a "spiritual" one is still seeking. Changing the direction of your running on the wheel does not get you off it, it merely breaks the monotony while reinforcing the sense of someone who is seeking. Seeking is intrinsically hopeless; it does not sustain happiness. Being happy is the antithesis of seeking; neither one can generate or sustain the other. It is so simple. The absence of one is the presence of the other. To be free of the search is to be free of what causes it: the fear and suffering inherent in separative life.

Working with Self Hatred

The first approach to working with self hatred is that we find all the things about ourselves that are loveable: we are a good partner, a good parent, a good musician. And, we put attention on those things and reason it out: I'm not a bad person; my children love me. Or we try various therapeutic processes.

The other approach is that in the ultimate view of reality there is no one to love and nothing to love, so what is the problem? So you explode the whole thing; and what you find is love—not anything or someone *to* love, but just Love. We resist that because body, emotions and mind have a certain reason for existence that we protect and defend at all costs. The raison d'etre of emotions is to bring some kind of harmony to the system, as strange as it seems! One of the primal drives of the system is love, love in human terms. Then we find the Path, and the Path is about love—not loving, or being loved, but Love. In the process of here and now there is just what is . . . So, just Love.

Are We Having Fun Yet?

It's a sign of great maturity when you can have fun with your parents.

Hope and Hopelessness

———

When you define any characteristic or quality, you automatically imply its opposite. You can't just hope. You can't under any circumstances have only one side of the equation. When there is hope, the implication is that hopelessness is there. You may not be feeling it or recognizing it, but it's there, and sooner or later you're going to hit hopelessness. Hope is natural to the human mind. To deal with hope *as it is* is to accept the reality of hope and the reality of hopelessness. It doesn't mean that hopelessness is necessarily going to manifest or overtake you, but it's there.

For most of us, when we're committed to one side of the equation, we're resisting the other side of the equation. If someone is sick and you're praying for them to get well, it means you're resisting them not getting well, or getting worse. When you accept the reality that there is hope *and* hopelessness in the dualistic world, it completely harmonizes the energy that you've constellated around either of those two positions. When the energy is harmonized, it takes away the implications, the consequences. It simply leaves it *as it is*. Then there is hope, there is hopelessness, and what arises arises.

Vow to Conquer Illusion

Are you clear enough, discriminating enough, and disciplined enough to make sane, adult, mature choices (with regard to Internet usage and technology) and maintain those choices in the face of a vibrantly seductive, fame-and-fortune-promising mirage? Well, future Bodhisattvas all, remember when you take the vow you will intone: "Illusion is endless, I vow to conquer it all." That refers to your own illusion—imagining yourselves to be competent enough to have answered "Yes, of course" to that last question—as you can't conquer the illusion of anyone else, only *they* can, although you can apply a bit of pressure to the fissures here and there.

How Change Comes

———

We have this idea—"I want to change, to be more alive, happy."
You have to accept yourself as you are, as if the way you are at
this very moment is *never* going to change. What that does is
gives the power of change to our *being* and takes it away from
ego. Ego has the power to change, but will never do it. Real
change comes from *being*. Continue to observe yourself as
you are with this qualification: Any judgment—good, bad, et
cetera—or expectation of yourself to change stops the process
of change. If change is going to come, it comes from relaxing
our chokehold, our grip, on just letting things be as they are
right here, right now.

Look to Children to Lead the Way

One of the impersonal values of having children in our lives may be to show us how "unwhole" we are. Because children touch our hearts so deeply, the sorrow of realizing the illnesses of the world based on recognizing what that is to children—how war, greed, cruelty, torture and criminal atrocities affect them—can really spur us on to investigate what it means to be completely whole and conscious ourselves. If one really feels the nature of human suffering, and if one looks at an innocent child who doesn't know anything about the realities of all of that (they just play and they eat and they cry and they laugh), and if one thinks of what it is going to cost for that child to lose their innocence, if that's not enough of a burr under the saddle to motivate us to want to come out of hiding and to become conscious (to mature in our spiritual and temporal life), nothing ever will be. As long as the child still maintains some innocence, every expression of this innocence should be such a reminder.

More Important than the Lie

One of the many instructions for practice in the Gurdjieff Work is to not manifest negative emotion. Imagine if you were given an exercise to live for just *two weeks* without manifesting any negative emotions: criticism, annoyance, irritation, impatience, anger, vanity, shame, greed, pride. Imagine the kind of internal pressure that would build up. When ego is not allowed to express itself in its habitual way—not allowed to control the situation—it starts getting nervous, and it starts doing stupid things. There are circumstances in the Work that are intentionally designed to put ego in a compromising situation, so that it shows us something about ourselves that we have been unwilling to see up to that point. In order to profit from that kind of Paying Attention, awakening has to be more important to us than sleep; the truth has to be more important to us than the lie.

Embrace the Miraculous

———

To ultimately "make it" in this work of awakening, of transformation, you have to embrace the miraculous—always. And that miracle is being so much at peace with yourself that you can turn your energy towards welcoming and using the opportunities that are always falling into your lap. To embrace and devour these opportunities will make you free, happy, full of life and passion. Then your circumstances won't affect you so dramatically. It is the nature of this work that a revelation, a breakthrough, could happen at any time, and has many times! But, how easily we forget.

Handling Our Demons

Here is a clear description of how to handle your own demons: watch, do not indulge, do not distract yourself, do nothing. And what happens? The demons crawl back into their cave. And yes, they will rise again, and if you respond to them in exactly this way—watch, do not indulge, do not distract yourself, do nothing—they will crawl away hungry and dissatisfied again and again. And at some point, they will stop rising with any degree of force and even that will be rarely, if at all. But you must stay with it and you must not crack, for once you go back to the old habits, "eat, drink, movie, shop" etc. ... they know they still have you and will continue to assault you, even if you successfully ignore them randomly. You must be tenacious and absolutely consistent, like an addict denying the addiction to get its claws back in. And like an addiction, it pays to have a "sponsor," someone, many someones, who you trust and who can give you good counsel. And it also pays to avoid the enabler (don't go back to the old neighborhood).

Get a Sense of the Changeless

Dark moods come and go, bright moods come and go. Things that we take very seriously one morning, a week later we have completely forgotten. If we can get a sense of that, the constant volatility and movement of form, of externals, then we also get a sense of that which is changeless and formless—that point of absolute stillness, balance, harmony. That is the point that is never out of harmony because it is always one with *what is*.

Our Greatest Contribution

The greatest contribution we can make to the Universe is not a function of our intelligence, our creative skills, or our capacity to produce. We want to serve the Universe by writing the perfect song, or painting the perfect picture, or coming up with the greatest invention for serving human comfort. We don't want to realize that the greatest form of help we can offer the Universe may be something as nebulous as having compassion for others. We just don't want to realize that, because we're too attached to our identification with the personal elements of our existence. But maybe that's it—the most profound way we can practice and serve the Universe is to feel compassion for others.

Invitation to Work

There was a man at the Prieuré when Gurdjieff was there. He was a cranky Russian man. Nobody liked him; he was always angry, always critical, impossible to deal with. One day, people became so aggressive toward this man that he left the Prieuré. He was on his way to Paris to get a job when Gurdjieff found out what had happened, chased the guy down and talked him into coming back. When everybody else came to Gurdjieff and said, "We were finally rid of this guy! Why did you bring him back? You know what he is like," Gurdjieff said, "Yes, I know exactly what he's like, that's why I pay him to stay here."

Why We Work

What interests me is that about you which is never out of communication with the Divine. But the unfortunate thing about us as individuals is this: What is never out of communication with the Divine is almost always out of communication with our faculty of attention. Thus the need for work. Spiritual work is not a quick answer to cleaning up the mess that our lives are in. Real spiritual work is never about what we can produce for ourselves, but rather what we can produce *out of ourselves* for something higher. The point of spiritual work is to serve God. If in serving God the messes we have made of our lives clear up—great, wonderful. If the messes we have made of our lives do not clear up, and in fact get worse—well, blame God, go on, and keep working.

335

So Simple

―――――

All you have to do is, for one instant, stop fighting to sustain your separation, and there is only what is. It is quite simple.

Crushed by Love
(for Yogi Ramsuratkumar)

So You, Madman,
　　is this one of Your celebrated Sins?
You have broken lee's heart
　　and now You break his mind?
I will not run from You
　　for are You not my Father?
In fact I will sacrifice myself willingly
　　into Your equally willing embrace.
Yes, oh dirty Beggar,
　　I am beyond tests and trials.
You are making Your son
　　as Mad as You.
lee throws himself headlong
　　at Your dusty Feet
and thanks You for crushing him
　　until there is nothing but You.
You make the sweetest wine
　　of very sour grapes.

Prayer Is Praise

———

We often don't know whether Faith is true of us or not until circumstances prove so or not.

What to do? Prayer is always a reliable process. Not the kind of supplication that asks for Faith, but simply Praise; pure Praise for no reason, or if we want to call it a reason, simply to proclaim the Glory of God. Such prayer is never wasted. It always bears fruit, even if we are unaware of it. You can and you may always resort to prayer. You don't need a formula, just start praising the Mercy and Majesty of God and pour it on. It may be a bit embarrassing, but persist; the merits are great and there is no downside. And keep it to yourself.

Hopefully, the opportunities to test your Faith will be mild and few and far between. After all, there is no need to wish to suffer great trials only to discover whether this elusive Faith is established in us. Glorify the Radiant and Bright Lord above all else, and no matter what anyone thinks (even you), you will be Blessed, all the way to the bank, as they say.

Only Practice Is Reliable

To accept what is, as it is, here and now . . . Just This. It is the only thing that is absolutely reliable, no matter how much beauty we have in our lives, even if what we do brings us joy. Practice is the only thing that is absolutely reliable. Everything else passes; everything else passes. What if you get Alzheimer's—all of the wonderful memories, everything is gone! Everything passes in the material world. The subtle domains are also material. Only practice, through birth and death, time and space—only practice is reliable.

No Top End

There is no "end of the road." The worst possible situation a spiritual student can get into is assuming that he or she is "done" and they can now discontinue all of their spiritual practices and Work. This encourages stagnation, which soon turns everything into poison and rotten garbage.

340

Tantra Is

———

The traditional practice of tantra essentially means meeting and going through the elements of the underworld converting these elements rather than attempting to escape them or ignore them, as a way to realization. We need fear, desires, illnesses, greed, possessiveness and all of the life-negative qualities that each of us has to some degree, and through working with them we transform them. Even if we didn't need them, they are an integral part of us, and must be recognized. But we *do* need them. They help make up who we are in the upperworld. Without them, we would not be human and therefore would not have the Divine possibility and Divine opportunity that human existence is. Through working *with* these forces, not in spite of them, they are transformed. That's essentially what tantra is.

What Creates Disharmony

What creates disharmony is separating that which is not separate. That separation can only take place in the mind, because in reality we cannot separate that which is not separate. The Buddhists use the word, "Buddhamind," for Reality, which means seeing things as they are and accepting them, because the mind, isolated from the rest of the body, can *see* things as they are, but mind cannot *accept* things as they are. The mind creates separation. When we are measuring what is against what was or could be, of course there is disharmony.

Jesus Loved God

———

Jesus loved God, and he was never distracted by anything. He lived an ordinary life, eating, sleeping, interacting with his disciples. He lived in the world; he was flesh and blood. And even though he lived in the world, he never allowed the world to distract him. He was always perfectly turned to God. After his death, the disciples were distracted by the fact that the master was gone: "What are we going to do without the master?" The fact of his being resurrected and coming back to his disciples was to say, "Look, there is only God. So how come there is no God anymore as soon as I'm gone? You're distracted. Just turn to the Lord." He didn't come back in order to show them that it was possible to attain personal immortality. It was always God.

Rise and Fall

———

When you accept what is, as it is, across the spectrum, essentially you are turning life over to the Divine. You're essentially moving out of the realm of your past and the possibility of your future, in terms of how it affects your consciousness, according to the way you want it to fall out. You are basically saying to the Divine, "Okay, You move things. You create." Under that circumstance, hope may still arise, but it is arising in a system in which whatever arises falls into the same category. It arises, you notice it, it subsides. The way we usually are is that something arises, and if it's something that we want, we immediately grab hold of it. Then we are taking over the work of the Universe. When we accept what is, as it is, here and now, we have disengaged our spatial and temporal relationship to duality—which is always a function of the past or the future, of hope or fear—and we just surrender to the Universe.

Others Help Us

———

In one sense we literally *rely* on the transformation of others to give our transformational-impetus fuel. Without the influence of those who have gone before us, the mechanics of transformation can only be relatively effective, but combined with that influence the mechanics can be very, very important. In Zen, even after someone has this transformation from *no* to *yes,* they still continue to practice, they still continue to sit. Enlightenment (or transformation) goes on by itself, and it also has to be anchored in life. In Zen they don't practice in order to keep their satori in place as a mechanical act, they practice to honor the tradition, to bring dignity and respect to the tradition. And it is the personal values of honor, dignity and respect, and their ongoing integral activity that sustain the transformation.

Ordinary Magic

Don't cultivate the need for certainty. Cultivate receptivity, maybe with a touch of wonder. In Tibetan there's a word *drala*, which translates very loosely as "ordinary magic." What it means, also very loosely translated, is that in every moment of life there is the possibility for magic; and magic is translated as the immediacy of the presence of reality, here and now.

"Magic" doesn't mean some fantastic occurrence—lightning storms, and angels flying around your head whispering in your ear. The way Tantric practitioners of Tibetan Buddhism use that word, magic is exactly *the acceptance of what is, as it is, here and now*. And they call that *drala*.

In that acceptance there is wonder and magic. Anything is possible! The expanse of life opens up in front of you, instead of closing down to a tiny aperture. When possible, it helps to cultivate a sense of the possibility of life, rather than the oppressiveness of life; to cultivate the possibility of wonder in every moment.

Remove the Clutter

———

What does it mean to remove your own clutter? Well, clearly we aren't just talking about the external stuff you might be weighed down with, electronically and virtually, like your unnecessary but addictive ego-stroking and ego-satisfying internet projects. We are also talking about all of the psychic/psychological blood suckers—the parasites of mind, cells, and soul—that are leeching you dry and effectively keeping you exactly where you are, unable to move even a millimeter. You know, all the "I couldn't help myself" junk, all the overbearing emotional states, the clinging to childhood dynamics and antiquated survival strategies and so on and so on. Can you do this? The answer, which I bet you guessed I was going to say, is: Yes, you can.

The Real Sign of Practice

—▼—

Meditation and study are something anyone can do. The *real* sign of practice is kindness, skillful means, forbearance and sensitivity with others.

Power for Transformation

We live in a very dynamic Universe. Most people live in a singular Universe—only one reality. Even though the Universe is always trying to convey its multiple forms, we keep going back to the view that there is only one reality. The gross physical world of the five senses is not the only reality. You've got to be able to shift realities instantly, because we live in a dangerously shifting, changing world, and you don't want to be stuck in a five-sense, space/time reality if you don't have to be.

The more subtle the realities are, the more power they have. Money, for example, is just a metaphor, a symbol for power, and power is what tantra is about—power used for the Work, not power used for what you think is useful. If you go to India and meet tantric sadhus, most of them are angry and unhappy, because they misunderstand the aim of power. They seek to be yogis with personal power, which is why they're angry. Those tantric sadhus who understand that they are gathering power for the impersonal purpose of the transformation of humankind are relaxed and attractive.

You Just Might Not Know

The difficulty we have with practice is that the results are often so subtle we don't even know there have been any. Eventually we know, but "eventually" could be on our deathbed: There we are dying, and we realize that our practice was fabulously successful, even though we were always extremely self-critical. What's needed is to practice without basing the vigor of your practice on your *concept* of what the result would look like, because most of us don't know what it would look like.

Drawing the Attention of the Divine

Everything in the Universe expands and contracts. Why should our relationship to the Divine be any different? When we move into a period of contraction, we shouldn't say "What did I do wrong?" Expansion and contraction balance each other. We need to view our sadhana that way so we don't waste our energy dealing with these natural states. If everything in the Universe kept expanding, it would blow up and there would be infinite contraction. These opposites are the wings that carry us to the Divine. When we're in a state of ecstasy and expansion, we draw the attention of the Divine. When we're in a state of separation, and we're cursing and imploring God, if the fear and pain of separation is acute, it's another form of prayer and we're drawing the attention of the Divine to us.

Keep Energy Moving

———◆———

It's very healthy, given the laws of energy, to keep the energy moving. Whether the energy is love, or good vibes, or money, energy demands movement so that things don't stagnate and rot. Money is a wonderful thing if you use it! Storing it away for a rainy day, saving things to use later, often doesn't work out the way you think it's going to.

Money is most effective when it is active, when it is doing something. The more active movement the better. Nature abhors a vacuum—money is energy, and energy is always returned to you when you use it. When you spend money, it is always returned to you, but not necessarily in the form of money. Energy is returned to you in the form of love or friendship. So, it's good to keep money moving, obviously with intelligence. If you get ahead of yourself, it can be counterproductive. If you want to go out of business quickly, be fanatical about the details.

Bad News

The source of social breakdown: white middle-class workaholics, stressed to the point of epidemic child abuse, wielding power to destroy any shreds of honor and integrity left at the levels of responsible government and industry, and incapable of love, tenderness, and even minimal feeling in relationship, both within family and in the greater circle of human society.

There is not one rotten apple in the barrel. There are only one or two healthy applies left in the barrel and they must be taken out and protected and the whole barrel thrown in the compost. I don't have any faith that this will be done, but I do have faith in the natural evolutionary fact that when everything rots, it eventually turns to fertilizer in which fresh new growth is assured (as long as the seeds are allowed to remain). In any case one thing we can be assured of is that if there is a last laugh it will be God laughing it and that is, in the end, our true salvation.

Good News

The good news is Yogi Ramsuratkumar. The good news is the brilliant green of each new shoot of plant life. The good news is the pure clarity and innocence in the infants' eyes. The good news is the Work is alive and well in small and not so small enclaves of practice and dedication, devotion and sacrifice, in every corner of the world, deep in the bowels of every race and every religion. The good news is that God has already had the last laugh and it's a sparkling burst of delight over the "success" of His creation, over the final victory of His eternal consort, Shakti. Amen.

Life Is about Transformation

It's our job to die every day—to die in the master, to die in the Work—so that our illusions do not overwhelm the impulse to live a life of genuine honesty and truth, because typically they do. We are very sincere people, but we're creatures of habit, and it's very difficult to break that structure.

You've got to manage your mind, emotions and body, because if they have anything to say, you will not make the transition. And you've got to make the transition, because your life is not about your beautiful children, or your hungry sex, which is equally beautiful; or about political consciousness, or your wish for stability and peace in the world, although we should always fight for justice. What life is about is transformation. What life is for is to move transformationally forward, evolutionarily. You must make the transition, because this is what your life is about. Your life has led you to this point.

Begging for Poverty
(for Yogi Ramsuratkumar)

For so long I sought riches,
    and found much wealth
till I discovered You,
    a Beggar,
and now seek only the Poverty
    You so regally bear.
To be as Poor as You,
    Beloved Guru,
is a blessing I only dream of
    with awe.
So sings Lee, his wealth effaced
    in the Poverty of his Lord.
May this only be so.

The Eyes to See

Parvati to Shiva: "Everybody's talking about you as this great devotional God, but you're just absorbed in yourself here, not doing anything! Why don't you go down there and serve some people?" So, Shiva thought he would teach Parvati a lesson. He took a big sack of gold, and he threw it down to earth. *Bang*! The gold falls right in the middle of a public thoroughfare, waiting for the lucky devotee of Shiva who will come along and find it. Meanwhile, there's a man walking along, dragging his crippled leg, and complaining, "Oh, why did God give me this leg? Look at all the healthy people around. Why couldn't I have been healthier?" He's cursing Shiva, too. But then he gets this thought: "You know, things could be worse. I could be blind. Let me see how bad that would be," so he closes his eyes and pretends to be blind. Now, as he walks along the road with his eyes closed, he passes right by the sack of gold. Only when he passes the gold does he open his eyes again. Then Shiva says to Parvati, "There! Now you understand."

Prior to Woman's Fear

Receptivity is the major feminine disposition and fear is woman's dilemma. Find the root of the arising of this pervasive fear, and rest, or be conscious, there. Live there; dwell in that place. There is no "how to" instruction that is possible here. The only way to finally transcend the fear that underlies your life and prevents your femininity from expressing itself (and nothing else will deal with the fear except on a temporary basis) is to realize *what is prior to it,* and to live in that realization as your state of being.

Afraid of Sacrifice

———

We come to this Work and hear the word "sacrifice" and get very afraid we will lose everything. But our fear of sacrifice keeps us from a deeper intimacy with the Divine. Our fears are groundless. Yes, there is a transition from ego-centered to universality, but the things we are afraid of losing are not the things we have to sacrifice. We use those things we are afraid of sacrificing as an excuse to keep from committing to the Path.

Decide to See

———

There are things that we don't like about ourselves that we completely justify and excuse, but when we are talking about Paying Attention we have to see every quality of every moment clearly without denial or justification or analysis, without editorializing, without guilt or shame. The way Paying Attention begins is that we Pay Attention with the ego, and therefore we are going to be selective. We're going to see some things very clearly and some things we are not going to see at all. So, if we are committed to the practice of Paying Attention, we start there. How do we get committed to it? Make a decision. How do we know the decision is effective? It doesn't matter. If you are a man or woman of integrity, you make a decision and you just stick by your decision. How many of you, at random times in your life, have the urge to lie or steal, but you don't do it? It's not because you can't do it; it's not because you don't want to do it. It's because you made a decision that lying is not just. It's exactly the same with spiritual practice.

Give Your Life

The Work wants your life—but only when you are in a love affair with life itself, only when you are bright, strong, confident, capable, in short: ALIVE. The Work does not want some kind of dull, dispassionate, struggling, agonizing humanoid. To give your life to the Work is to give breath, passion and activity to the Work every day. You have to have a childlike, eternal *beginner's mind,* a belief in miracles, like, "Any day anything can happen!"

A Prayer of Adoration
(for Yogi Ramsuratkumar)

Oh my Darling
    Yogi Ramsuratkumar,
If I were a woman
    And You were a man
I would worship You
    And follow You to the ends of
                        the earth.

But alas
    Dearest One,
I am only an arrogant Fool
    and You are my Father.
So I will adore You
    and follow you to the
        beginnings of Love.

Practice Wears Down the Mind

———

When the sixteenth Karmapa was dying, he looked at his concerned disciples and said, "Nothing happens." What the Karmapa's disciples could do was consider: "How could he say 'Nothing happens' when he was dying?" Good question! Maybe that's why he said that—to give them that kind of rub. If they were serious, they would solve the *koan* of "Nothing happens." Doing that, they would completely contextualize mind and emotions, which were obviously *not* running the Karmapa's consciousness, in any way.

Practice wears down the mind. Remembrance wears down the mind. Every time you remember, every time you remember to chant, to practice inquiry, you are wearing down the mind. The mind is a forgetting machine when it comes to practice. Just remembering is a tremendously effective practice, which is why we say "Pay attention and Remember." And, there is "Remember" with a capital *R* and "remember" with a small *r*. The practice is about both levels.

Stop Being Everyone Else

It's important to distinguish between hormonal demands and conscious demands . . . Self-observation is the way we make those distinctions. We need to have a real, active sense of ourselves, physically, emotionally, mentally and spiritually. If you're ever going to be authentically yourself, the first thing you have to do is stop being everyone else.

Designing Good Citizens

Human society, as it is now, has "designed" our minds to make sure that we are completely divorced from our heart—uninformed by any kind of sanity or intelligence or wisdom, or joy. People who live by their hearts don't necessarily make good citizens, and what every government wants is good citizens. People who live by their hearts, however, if they disagree with the government, are able to act in ways that demonstrate their own sense of integrity.

365

Guru's Blessing

May we, all beings, be happy and fulfilled in Dharma, Buddha, Sangha, and Guru (even the Guru!), and may the joy and power of the Blessings of Yogi Ramsuratkumar flow unimpeded like the Ganges in monsoon, and may the opulence, the *pushti* of our service to Krishna, and therefore to Self, never wane, never waver, never be in doubt or conflict. May we abandon ourselves to ourselves, Realizing only God, the other, and "Just This," and may all Divine beings celebrate our Guru Yoga and pour their Benediction upon us and ours like honey gushing from an overfull hive. And may we live lives of fulfillment, creativity, deep satisfaction and profound value and profit to the Work. And may every child, adult, and elder smile at you, knowing and seeing your transcendental and your emanent beauty, delight, and perfection. In fact, may delight and joy plague you unavoidably, and may you never suffer unnecessarily, having embodied fully all of this, my wishes for you. I bow to you with hands folded, forehead to the ground and eternity before us.

Abbreviations for Sources

IF	*In the Fire*
IS	*Intimate Secrets of a True Heart Son: Poems and Prayers to Yogi Ramsuratkumar*
LBL	*The Little Book of Lies and Other Myths* (Journal 5)
LS	*Laughter of the Stones*
LGB	*Living God Blues*
LLP	Lee Lozowick Project, "Live in Europe" CD
MAN	Mangalam, Canada, 1999 seminar transcriptions
MSE	*In the Mood of, In the Style of Eccentricities* (Journal 3)
OG	*The Only Grace Is Loving God*
SCF	*A Small Collection of Feuilletons by One of the Rasnochintsy* (Journal 6)
SE	*In the Style of Eccentricities . . .* (Journal 2)
SSB	Spiritual Slavery, Biography
TAV	Tavern (late night tea space) discourse
TTI	*A Tale Told by an Idiot Full of Sound and Fury . . .* (Journal 7)
TW	*Tawagoto*
WFF	*Words of Fire and Faith*
WII	*What Is Is*, Mangalam seminar, transcripts 2001
YE	*The Yoga of Enlightenment/The Book of Unenlightenment*
ZT	*Zen Trash*

Sources

Dedication: ALS,
  280-281
1. HSM, FJ, 11
2. WFF, 69-70
3. LBL, 78
4. AII, 703
5. CP, 1
6. SCF, 101
7. DT, 1995
8. CR, 126
9. LBL, 77
10. DT, 7-25-86
11. CR, 144-145
12. CBP, 347
13. AII, 702
14. CP, 49-50
15. *Esotera*, German
  magazine, June
  1986
16. WFF, 117-118
17. LBL, 159-160
18. WFF, 25-26
19. IF, 46
20. AT, 49-50
21. HSM, PC, 209
22. DDM, 189-190
23. HSM, PC, 83
24. TTI, 159, 160
25. ED, 169
26. HSM, PC, 41-42
28. WFF, 59

29. TW, vol. 19, no.
  2, 138
30. AII, 362
31. ED, 146
32. TTI, 35, 36
33. AII, 664
34. HSM, HV, 58
35. GR, 37
36. ALS, 127-128
37. LLP, "Live in
  Europe"
38. CBP, 471, 473
39. GR, 70-71
40. Haus Schnede
  seminar, 1990
41.WFF, 17
42. HSM, HV, 191
43. FF, 102-104
44. YE, 79
45. TTI, 84
46. AII, 369
47. ED, 173
48. TTI, 97
49. CBP, 23
50. SCF, 63-64
51. TW, vol. 24, no.
  1, 56
52. ED, 146
53. WFF, 104-105
54. AII, 703
55. WFF, 57

56. EIS, 184
57. CR, 130
58. ALS, 54, 55
59. HSM, LR, 170
60. WFF, 150
61. YE, 94
62. LGB, 57-58
63. CP, 51-52
64. AII, 368
65. CR, 51-52
66. ALS, 70
67. SCF, 31
68. AII, 771
69. TAV, 12-27-85
70. AII, 333
71. HSM, HV, 191-192
72. SCF, 117, 119
73. WII
74. CBP, 111
75. AII, 275
76. Meal prayer, Hohm
  Community
77. WFF, 13
78. YE, 105
79. ADT, late 1980s
80. LGB, 137
81. IF, 8
82. LBL, 78
83. HSM, HV, 64
84. ALS, 130
85. SCF, 91

86. TTI, 230
87. WFF, 141
88. SCF, 23
89. TTI, 223-224
90. YE, 51
91. ED, 294
92. HSM, FJ, 198
93. MSE, 33
94. Arizona Celebration invitation, April 1993
95. AII, 703
96. DDM, 302
97. ALS, 53
98. ED, 23
99. CYT, 198
100. HSM, PC, 216
101. LS, 69-70
102. TTI, 147, 148
103. ALS, 8
104. HSM, PC, 42
105. AT, 2
106. LBL, 225
107. WFF, 192-193
108. HSM, France, 181
109. CR, 218
110. WFF, 127
111. LBL, 144-145
112. WFF, 201-202
113. CR, 124
114. TTI, 92
115. ED, 54
116. ED, 173
117. ALS, 104
118. WFF, 13
119. SCF, 40
120. LGB, 144
121. HSM, NPV, 64
122. MAN
123. AII, 425
124. HSM, PC, 40-41
125. ALS, 69
126. ALS, 10
127. GAV, 699
128. AII, 275
129. WFF, 183
130. AII, 339
131. CR 128-129
132. TTI, 202
133. SCF, 25
134. AT, 113-114
135. HSM, NPV, 369
136. WFF, 240
137. AII, 382-383
138. AII, 370
139. HSM, PC, 144-145
140. TW, vol. 19, no. 2, 132
141. WFF, 55
142. MSE, 89
143. AII, 425-426
144. AII, 387-388
145. TTI, 66
146. YE, 69
147. IS, 595
148. CBP, 650
149. HSM, PC, 41
150. HSM, HV, 80
151. AII, 329
152. HSM, PC, 207-208
153. SCF, 17
154. ALS, 250-251
155. TW, vol. 19, no. 2, 132
156. ED, 306-307
157. ALS, 15-16
158. ALS, 55
159. CYT, 216
160. CYT, 74
161. SCF, 28-29
162. FF, 142
163. ALS, 20
164. ALS, 14-15
165. TTI, 222
166. CYT, 71
167. HSM, FJ, 221
168. SSB, BOOK 3, 139
169. CYT, 216
170. ED, 197
171. HSM, PC, 220
172. YE, 99
173. AII, 365
174. DDM, 569
175. HSM, LR, 170
176. WFF, 57
177. BP, 177
178. HSM, PC, 206
179. LGB, 126
180. CBP, 152
181. TW, vol. 25, no. 2, 13
182. DT, 8-3-86
183. WFF, 237
184. ALS, 113
185. LGB, 41-142

186. WFF, 41-42
187. ED, 294-295
188. TTI, 209
189. GR, 76
190. LGB, 108
191. IS, 613
192. MSE, 45
193. WFF, 142
194. IF, 107
195. CBP, 159
196. MSE, 29
197. IF, 29
198. EIS, 80-81
199. HSM, NPV, 184
200. DDM, 278
201. AG, 7, 6
202. ED, 304
203. WFF, 40
204. LGB, 141
205. HSM, NPV, 368
206. SCF, 99
207. CBP, 347
208. CBP, 179
209. CYT, 189-190
210. CP, 1
211. Tavern invitation, early 1980s.
212. WFF, 104-105
213. IF, 214
214. LBL, 7
215. TW, vol. 24, no. 1, 41
216. WFF, 186-187
217. ED, 191-92
218. ALS, 102, 114

219. WFF, 194-195
220. AII, 333-334
221. GR, 63-64
222. AII, 394
223. AT, 124-125
224. CBP, 146-147
225. WFF, 171
226. TTI, 85-86
227. HSM, PC, 148
228. FF, 177-178
229. AII, 359
230. HSM, NPV, 184
231. WFF, 13
232. WFF, 76-77
233. AG, 28-29
234. SCF, 60
235. FF, 111
236. FF, 34-35
237. AII, P. 367
238. HSM, FJ, 222
239. ALS, 12-13
240. CP, 237
241. GR, 16
242. WFF, 20
243. LGB, 145
244. ED, 175
245. OG, 73-74
246. CYT, 122
247. TTI, 60-61
248. DDM, 340
249. MSE, 8-9
250. HSM, HV, 63
251. CR, 159-160
252. CBP, 11
253. CBP, 151-152

254. YE, 56
255. CR, 126
256. YE, 31
257. HSM, FJ, 11.
258. FF, 176
259. LGB, 136
260. ALS, 52
261. AII (page unknown)
262. ALS, 48
263. AG, 5
264. MSE, 46-47
265. CBP, 118
266. AII, 295
267. CR, 127
268. GR, 34
269. HSM, PC, 240
270. AT, 45-46
271. AT, 37
272. WFF, 14
273. WFF, 117
274. SCF, 81-82
275. AII, 251
276. LGB, 108
277. SCF, 52
278. CBP, 581-582
279. IS, 189
280. WFF, 94
281. CR, 153
282. DDM, 498
283. WFF, 76
284. IF, 192
285. HSM, HV, 58
286. FF, 113
287. IF, 190
288. CBP, 23

289. TTI, 200
290. YE, 77-78
291. AII, 386-387
292. ALS, 150-151
293. AG, 41
294. WFF, 56
295. YE, 3
296. AII, 423
297. BU, 82-83
298. DT, 11-25-84
299. TTI, 230
300. ED, 197
301. SCF, 92
302. CBP, 273
303. ALS, 117
304. SCF, 9-10
305. ED, 305
306. SCF, 21
307. SCF, 67
308. FF, 127-128
309. AII, 528
310. SCF, 37
311. LGB, 147
312. MAN
313. CP, 69
314. ZT, 3-4
315. BU, 94-95
316. SCF, 78

317. ED, unpublished
    version
318. ALS, 274
319. WFF, 76-77
320. DDM, 337
321. IF, 52
322. CBP, 141
323. DT, 5-29-84
324. GR, 65-66
325. TTI, 159
326. AII, 283
327. CP, 7
328. HSM, 217-218
329. ALS, 38, 41
330. CYT, 177-178
331. AII, 330-331
332. ED, 301
333. HSM, FJ, 212
334. AT, 1-2
335. IF, 96
336. DDM, 540
337. WFF, 86-87
338. CBP, 153
339. YE, 70
340. ALS, 196
341. AII, 331
342. IF, 174-175
343. GR, 67-68

344. AII, 333
345. FF, 114
346. WFF, 38-39
347. HSM, 185
348. CBP, 378-381
349. TW, vol. 22, no.
    3, 72
350. TW, vol. 25, no.
    2, 70
351. CBP, 428
352. MSE, 57
353. MSE, 58
354. CBP, 258-259
355. DDM, 204
356. ZT, 29-30
357. ALS, 13
358. HSM, HV, 192
359. HSM, PC, 216
360. ALS, 38, 41
361. DDM, 332
362. TW, vol. 19, no.
    2, 129
364. TW, vol. 22, no.1,
    25
365. WFF, 199-200

Bibliography and References

Books by Lee Lozowick

Acting God . . ., Prescott Valley, Arizona: Hohm Press, 1980

The Alchemy of Love and Sex, Prescott, Arizona: Hohm Press, 1996

The Alchemy of Transformation, Prescott, Arizona: Hohm Press, 1996

Cheating Buddha, Tabor, New Jersey: Hohm Press, 1980

Conscious Parenting, Revised Edition, Prescott, Arizona: Hohm Press, 2010

Death of a Dishonest Man: Poems and Prayers to Yogi Ramsuratkumar, Prescott, Arizona: Hohm Press, 1998

Feast or Famine: Teachings on Mind and Emotions, Prescott, Arizona: Hohm Press, 2008

Gasping for Air in a Vacuum: Poems and Prayers to Yogi Ramsuratkumar, Prescott, Arizona: Hohm Press, 2004

Getting Real, Prescott, Arizona: Hohm Press, 2007

In The Fire, Tabor, New Jersey: Hohm Press, 1978

Intimate Secrets of a True Heart Son: Poems and Prayers to Yogi Ramsuratkumar, Prescott, Arizona: Hohm Press, 2012

Laughter of the Stones, Tabor, New Jersey: Hohm Press, 1979-1980

Living God Blues, Prescott Valley, Arizona: Hohm Press, 1984

The Only Grace Is Loving God, Prescott Valley, Arizona: Hohm Press, 1982

Words of Fire and Faith: A View from the Edge, Prescott, Arizona: Hohm Press, 2013

The Yoga of Enlightenment/The Book of Unenlightenment, Prescott Valley, Arizona: Hohm Press, 1980

Other Books

Lee Lozowick, with commentary by Sylvan Incao, *Zen Trash: Irreverent & Sacred Teaching Stories of Lee Lozowick,* Prescott, Arizona: Hohm Press, 2002

Lee Lozowick and M. Young, *Enlightened Duality,* Prescott, Arizona: Hohm Press, 2009

Books by M. Young

As It Is: A Year on the Road with a Tantric Teacher, Prescott, Arizona: Hohm Press, 2000

Caught in the Beloved's Petticoats: A Treatise on the Eternal Way, Prescott, Arizona: Hohm Press, 2006

Spiritual Slavery: A Biography of Lee Lozowick, Vol. 1, the Years of Milk and Honey—1975–1980, Prescott, Arizona, 2011

Journals of Lee Lozowick

Eccentricities, Idiosyncrasies, and Sacred Utterances Of A Contemporary Western Baul (April 24, 1990 through August 28, 1990), Prescott, Arizona: Hohm Press, 1991

In the Style of "The Eccentricities, Idiosyncrasies and Sacred Utterances Of A Contemporary Western Baul" (May 10, 1992 through July 17, 1992), Prescott, Arizona: Hohm Press, 1992

In the Mood of "In the Style of The Eccentricities, Idiosyncrasies and Sacred Utterances Of A Contemporary Western Baul" (October 31, 1993 through March 7, 1994), Prescott, Arizona: Hohm Press, 1994

Cranky Rants and Bitter Wisdom from One Considered Wise in Some Quarters (February 27, 2002 through May 12, 2002), Prescott, Arizona: Hohm Press, 2002

The Little Book of Lies and Other Myths (May 14, 2005 through July 19, 2005), Prescott, Arizona: Hohm Press, 2005

Chasing Your Tail: Notes That May Be Difficult to Follow On Subjects That May Be Difficult To Grasp (March 2, 2009 through September 4, 2009), Prescott, Arizona: Hohm Press, 2009

A Small Collection of Feuilletons by One of the Rasnochintsy (December 23, 2006 through May 23, 2008), Prescott, Arizona: Hohm Press, 2008

"A Tale Told by An Idiot, Full of Sound and Fury Signifying…" Something Far Too Important To Be Disregarded (In Spite of Shameful Syntax, Misspellings and Sentences Almost As Long as the Mississippi River) (January 9, 2009 through March 2, 2009), Prescott, Arizona: Hohm Press, 2009

Study Manuals

Hohm Sahaj Mandir Study Manual: A Handbook for Practitioners of Every Spiritual and/or Transformational Path, Volumes I-IV, Prescott, Arizona: Hohm Press, 1996 (vol. I-II); 2002 (volumes III-IV)

Music

Lee Lozowick Project, "Live in Europe," Released 2007, UPC# 700261233376

Appendix

Glossary of Terms
and Short Biographies of Notable Persons

Terms

Aikido: is a modern Japanese martial art developed by Morihei Ueshiba as a synthesis of his martial studies, philosophy, and religious beliefs. Aikido is often translated as "the way of unifying (with) life energy" or as "the way of harmonious spirit." Ueshiba's goal was to create an art that practitioners could use to defend themselves while also protecting their attacker from injury.

Ananda: bliss

Be (or being) One With: Be (or being) One With: a core teaching of Swami Prajnanpad; to "embrace the self evident truth of the present moment" (Arnaud Desjardins) without resistance; not a mental state, but a full merging with the arising experience, with no need to express it.

Brahma: within the Hindu trinity of Brahma, Vishnu and Shiva, Brahma is the Creator or Emanator, sometimes called the Lord of Light.

Context: the texture of any given manifestation; the matrix or field in which all specific events, objects, and all specific forms arise.

Cramp: emotional reactivity or recoil; particularly the form of reactivity to which each individual reverts when survival is challenged. Can also refer to the "primal cramp," activity based on the belief that one is separate from God.

Dharma: a Buddhist term which refers to the defined and formally-propagated spiritually lawful and right way to live. In English it can be translated as "the Teaching." In the Western Baul Way, the terms "Dharma" and "Teaching" are interchangable and refer to the perennial Teaching, which abides as objective truth or reality as it is found in the great spiritual traditions of the world, both ancient and contemporary. This term also refers to the written or spoken teaching of a spiritual Master, the philosophical argument of a spiritual Way.

Draw No Conclusions Mind: a primary teaching of Lee Lozowick's. A state of free clarity, in which mental assumptions are surrendered in favor of innocence. Draw No Conclusions Mind enables us to directly see/know what is wanted and needed without the intrusion of mind's motivations.

Ego: the thought pattern that ensures survival of the organically separate individual. In practical terms, it consistently oversteps this function and also aggressively maintains the "survival" of the exclusive perspective of self-reference.

Enquiry: one of the core practices in Lee Lozowick's Teaching protocol. A form of practice in which the statement, "Who am I kidding?" is randomly used to question any feeling, thought, or experience that arises. It is used to serve the possibility of piercing insight into the true nature of the material, mental and emotional realms.

Father: the first person of the Trinity in the Christian tradition; also, the honorific term that Yogi Ramsuratkumar used for God; also, Lee's devotional reference to Yogi Ramsuratkumar: for example, "O my Father."

Grace: in Lee's Teaching, it is a gift of God bestowed on those who are already surrendered to God's Will; also, characterizes the ultimate possibility of the human.

Gender cultures: based in the recognition of the uniquenesses and differences in the physical, emotional, mental and psycho-spiritual natures of men and women. A gender culture is developed through networks of support, intimacy, work and communication among members of that gender (or those who identify as that gender) to honor and foster the individual's access to role models, to serve as an energetic source of impression food, to catalyze the individual's highest potentials (radiance of being, building of being) and to provide a foundation of clarity and compassion in the building of relationships with others, regardless of gender.

Great Process of Divine Evolution: the Will of God. It is the ongoing Process of God, which includes everything seen and unseen including life from conception to death.

Gurdjieff work: *see* **Work** or **The Work**

Holy Ghost (Holy Spirit): the third person of the Trinity (Father, Son, Holy Ghost or Holy Spirit) within the Christian tradition; the force of Love; the love of the Father for the Son.

Identification: I-am-that; the belief that I am only the body or the body's processes or functions, or that I am my thoughts or opinions, my emotions, my accomplishments or my roles.

Kabbalah: *see* **Qabala**

Kundalini: a form of primal energy (or shakti) said to be located at the base of the spine. Different spiritual traditions teach methods of awakening kundalini for the purpose of reaching spiritual enlightenment and a range of supernormal powers.

Lineage: (*Parampara* in Sanskrit) denotes a succession of teachers and disciples. The word literally means "an uninterrupted row or series, order, succession, continuation, mediation, tradition." In the paramparā system, knowledge (in any field) is passed down (undiluted) through successive generations.

Mahasamadhi: the "Great Bliss"; a term used to describe the physical passing away of the body of a great saint, guru or siddha.

Men's culture: *see* **Gender culture**

Organic Innocence: the basic ground of being for all manifestation, both animate and inanimate; the essential intelligence of being or existence itself as it shows up in particularized forms.

Paying Attention: the act of focusing the mind, body, intention and feelings on an object or process. "Pay Attention and Remember" was one of Lee's earliest teachings and the phrase has become a slogan (antidote) to be used to call oneself back to the present moment.

Qabala (Kabbalah): an esoteric method, discipline and school of thought that originated in Judaism. A set of esoteric teachings meant to explain the relationship between an unchanging, eternal, and mysterious *Ein Sof* (infinity) and the mortal and finite universe (God's creation).

Sadhana: spiritual practice

Sadhu: one who has renounced all aspects of worldly life to practice sadhana

Samadhi: a state of union or absorption in the Ultimate Reality

Sangha: company, community, companions on the Path

Satsang: meeting with and being in the good company of other spiritual practitioners or devotees

Shakti: the Divine Feminine force of God, also called Devi; the Divine energy as it is manifested and present in each individual

Shiva: the third aspect of the Hindu trinity, with Brahma and Vishnu; Shiva is the Destroyer and regenerating force.

Son: the second person of the Trinity within Christianity, along with the Father and the Holy Ghost (Holy Spirit); also, Jesus Christ. Lee refers to himself as the son in relationship to his Father, Yogi Ramsuratkumar.

Tantra: literally means "expansion." Tantra views all facets of life as natural, but to be transformed and subsumed through spiritual practice.

Tavern of Ruin: a Sufi term applied to the gathering of lovers of God who assemble for the purpose of sharing their longing for the Beloved. In Lee's work, the Tavern was a late-night gathering space for sharing the good company of one's sangha mates in the mood of Remembrance of God.

Tree of Life: *Etz haChayim* in Hebrew, is a classic descriptive term for the central mystical symbol used in the Kabbalah of esoteric Judaism. The tree, visually or conceptually, represents a series of divine emanations God's creation itself, out of nothing; the nature of revealed divinity, the human soul, and the spiritual path of ascent by humanity.

Vishnu: the Sustainer, and second person of the Hindu trinity of Brahma, Vishnu and Shiva.

Will of God: the universal movement of the Divine in every moment. Also refers to the absolute primacy of the Divine as Reality or Truth.

Women's culture: *see* **Gender culture**

Work (or The Work): the Great Work of God (the Creator) in creation; a human's participation in that; conscious, intentional inner labor to observe oneself as one is, without judgment or trying to change what is observed; remembering oneself in the midst of daily life; voluntary suffering as a result of observing oneself without buffers, lying, blaming or justifying.

Notable Persons

Arnaud Desjardins (1925–2011) was a French author and a producer at the Office de Radiodiffusion Télévision Française from 1952 to 1974. He was one of the first high-profile practitioners of Eastern religion in France. He worked on television documentaries with many spiritual traditions unknown to some Europeans at the time, including Hinduism, Tibetan Buddhism, Zen, and Sufism from Afghanistan. A disciple of Swami Prajnanpad, Arnaud Desjardins was a much-respected friend of Lee Lozowick, who was invited (since the early 1990s) to give a yearly seminar at his ashrams in France.

E.J. Gold (1941–) is an artist, musician, healer, teacher and author of more than 50 books on spiritual and self-help subjects. Mr. Gold was a personal friend of Lee Lozowick's and the two spent time together, and also offered teachings together on numerous occasions during Lee's life. His books, particularly *The Joy of Sacrifice* and *The Human Biological Machine As a Transformational Apparatus* were highly recommended by Lee in his teaching work with his students. He lives in Nevada City, California.

G. I. Gurdjieff (1866?–1947) was an influential early 20th century mystic, philosopher, spiritual teacher and composer, of Armenian and Greek descent, born in Armenia under Russian rule. Gurdjieff taught that most humans do not possess a unified mind-body consciousness and thus live their lives in a state of hypnotic "waking sleep," but that it is possible to transcend to a higher state of consciousness and achieve full human potential. Gurdjieff described a method attempting to do so, calling the discipline "The Work" (connoting "work on oneself"). According to his principles and instructions, Gurdjieff's method for awakening one's consciousness unites the methods of the fakir, monk or yogi, and thus he referred to it as the "Fourth Way."

Ramana Maharshi (1879–1950) was a Hindu sage who resided for his adult life at an ashram (Ramanashram) at the base of Mt. Arunachala in Tiruvannamali, south India. World renowned, he attracted devotees from across the globe. He recommended self-enquiry as the principal means to remove ignorance and abide in Self-awareness, together with bhakti (devotion) or surrender to the Self.

Milarepa (1052–1135) is generally considered one of Tibet's most famous yogis and poets. He was a student of Marpa Lotsawa, and a major figure in the history of the Kagyu school of Tibetan Buddhism.

Swami Prajnanpad (1891–1974) of Channa Ashram, was one of the eminent disciples of Niralamba Swami, a great yogi and guru of India. He entered the life of sannyasa (renunciation) and became Niralamba Swami's disciple in 1924-25. Instead of giving religious discourses, his unique method of teaching involved one-to-one contact with his disciples and devotees. He was an astute psychoanalyst as well. His many notable disciples included the French spiritual teacher Arnaud Desjardins.

Nicholas Roerich (1874–1947) was a Russian painter, trained both as an artist and a lawyer. A widely educated and well-traveled man, his interests included literature, philosophy, archaeology, hypnosis and a variety of spiritual practices. His paintings are said to have a hypnotic expression. Roerich was a dedicated activist for the cause of preserving art and architecture during times of war and earned several nominations for the Nobel Peace Prize long list.

Chögyam Trungpa, Rinpoche (1939–1987) was a Buddhist meditation master and holder of both the Kagyu and Nyingma lineages. A scholar, teacher, poet and artist, he was recognized both by Tibetan Buddhists and other spiritual practitioners and scholars as a preeminent teacher of Tibetan Buddhism. A major figure in the dissemination of Tibetan Buddhism to the West, he founded Vajradhatu and Naropa University and established the Shambhala Training method. His dozens of books, which present a pristine dharma accessible to Westerners, were highly recommended by Lee Lozowick as a primary source of study for his students.

Sanatan Das Thakur, Baul (1923–2016) was born at Khulna, Bangladesh within a family that had embraced the Baul tradition for at least four previous generations. His initiatory guru was Nitai Khepa, and later the great Monohor Khepa gave him instruction in the intricacies of the music. Until his death he lived on a small ashram in Khoirboni, Bengal, with his wife Mirabai and an extended family. Students of Lee Lozowick visited his ashram on numerous occasions, and sponsored his trip to the States in 1993 for musical performances. Lee also spent time with him in Calcutta in 2009.

About Lee Lozowick

Born in New Jersey in 1943, Lee Lozowick burst onto the American spiritual scene in 1975 offering a genuine alternative to the new-age, fast-path promise of enlightenment under which contemporary seekers were laboring. To the hippies of the day, he proposed "spiritual slavery" as the way to fly. A spiritual slave, according to Lee, was one who had seen through the illusions of freedom of choice and had opted for the will of God, willingly surrendering his or her precious life for a Purpose.

Lee was a radical visionary who founded three ashrams (USA, France and India) and established the Baul Path in the